THE GOD

OUR HEAVENLY

FATHER

IN THE AGE OF
TERRORISM

RUSSELL R. STANDISH &
COLIN D. STANDISH

HARTLAND PUBLICATIONS

The Godhead Volumes

Volume 1: *The Godhead: One, Two, Three, or Four?*

Volume 2: *Our Heavenly Father in the Age of Terrorism*

Volume 3: *Our Saviour—Human, Divine, or Human-Divine?*

Volume 4: *The Holy Ghost—Power or Being?*

All emphasis in quotations added by the
authors unless otherwise indicated.

Cover design and layout: Greg Solie • AltamontGraphics.com
Preliminary text editing: Maurie Walters
Text editing and layout: Harvey Steck

Published by
Hartland Publications
PO Box 1, Rapidan, VA, 22733 USA
(540) 672–3566
Printed in the USA

ISBN # 987-1-60564-007-5

Contents

CHAPTER 1

What If Satan Were "God"?

T HE concept of two contrasting gods is not unique to Buddhism. It is the false foundation of most pagan religions, including Shintoism, Taoism, Zoroastrianism, Hinduism, and many very primitive religions in Africa, the Australian Aborigines, the American Indians, and both the north and south of the island nations of the South Pacific.

Satan seeks to take the role of the good and the bad god. The Scriptures declare that Satan will actually come as an angel of light, and he is referred to as the god of this world in Scripture. (See 2 Corinthians 11:14; 4:4)

> And no marvel; for Satan himself is transformed into an angel of light. (2 Corinthians 11:14)

> In whom the god of this world hath blinded the minds of them which believe not, lest the light of the glorious gospel of Christ, who is the image of God, should shine unto them. (2 Corinthians 4:4)

Thus pagan religions have developed symbols of balance. The original symbol of balance was the cross—the balance of the vertical and the horizontal. Because of its pagan roots in ancient Babylon, early Christians did not use the cross as the symbol of Christianity; rather, they used the fish as its symbol of Christianity. Colin has visited two sets of catacombs in Rome, which were constructed to protect the early Christians, and no crosses were evident in them, but carved fish were quite common. The guide assured Colin that he had been through all the caves, and there was no evidence of crosses.

Another balance symbol common in paganism is the swastika (sometimes called the broken cross). It is very commonly used in Buddhist temples and less commonly in Hindu temples. Colin visited one Buddhist temple in Sandakan in Sabah, a state of Malaysia. There were literally thousands of swastikas decorating that temple.

The Chinese/Korean yin-yang is a symbol of balance. So are the two Jewish stars—the six-pointed star of David (the balancing of two triangles) or the eight-pointed star of Solomon (the balancing of two squares). An Orthodox Rabbi told Colin that their origins were lost in antiquity. In reality, they were taken from ancient paganism. Hindus of the Indonesian island of Bali have pagan gods which each night are covered with clothes having the pattern of checkerboard designs—a symbol of balance. Hindus decorate some of their temples with hermaphrodite gods, half male, half female, half white, half black.

Remember that Satan's religion is not established upon evil but rather the knowledge of good and evil. (Genesis 2:17)

The Chinese have developed more than two hundred and seventy of these polar opposites, such as good and evil, truth and error, male and female, hot and cold, white and black, big and small, tall and short, heavy and light, young and old, happy and sad, light and darkness.

The Zoroastrian religion balances light and darkness, but God contrasts them, for He has

> . . . called you out of darkness into his marvellous light. (1 Peter 2:9)

God provides, through Christ, all which is needed to overcome evil with good, falsehood with truth, wrong with right, and darkness with light. There lies the contrast between the kingdom of God in contrast with the false religion of Satan. Yet today, the large proportion of Christians have accepted the Satanic concept of religion that one can continue to sin and yet be assured of salvation. This is the foundation of relational religion. It denies the power of Christ to keep us from falling into sin. It is Satan's counterfeit and will lead many deceived Christians to eternal destruction.

> Now unto him that is able to keep you from falling, and to present you faultless before the presence of his glory with exceeding joy. (Jude 1:24)

> Therefore if any man be in Christ, he is a new creature: old things are passed away; behold, all things are become new. (2 Corinthians 5:17)

> Having therefore these promises, dearly beloved, let us cleanse ourselves from all filthiness of the flesh and spirit, perfecting holiness in the fear of God. (2 Corinthians 7:1)

> For it is a shame even to speak of those things which are done of them in secret. But all things that are reproved are made manifest by the light: for whatsoever doth make manifest is light. Wherefore he saith, Awake thou that sleepest, and arise from the dead, and Christ shall give thee light. See then that ye walk circumspectly, not as fools, but as wise. (Ephesians 5:12–15)

Sin cannot remain in the heart and life of the truly converted Christian.

> If we confess our sins, he is faithful and just to forgive us our sins, and to cleanse us from all unrighteousness. (1 John 1:9)

During the twenty years Russell served as a consultant physician (internist) and medical administrator in Southeast Asia, half that period was devoted to Penang, the second largest city of Malaysia. On Burma Road, in that city, was a popular Buddhist temple. The temple possessed the usual array of images of Buddha and other idols. The attention of most of the foreign visitors to the temple was focused on two of the idols.

Running from the mouths of these two idols, which possess fierce, ugly visages, was opium. Devotees earnestly prayed before these two idols, waving joss-sticks as they prayed. These are the two devil-idols in the temple. The prayers of these supplicants were not lacking in earnestness, for they feared the devil "gods," pleading for them to cast no evil spells upon them. The believers equally prayed earnestly before the idols representing the good "gods," seeking the blessings of health and prosperity.

Buddhism is well aware of the presence in the universe of a loving God who pours out His blessings in love to His people. However, adherents to Buddhism also believe in an evil, vile, and vengeful god who seeks to afflict them and destroy them. That they worship the God of heaven through idols is a tragedy, for such worship is unacceptable to our Father in heaven, as Scripture fully attests.

> For ye know how we have dwelt in the land of Egypt; and how we came through the nations which ye passed by; and ye have seen their abominations, and their idols, wood and stone, silver and gold, which were among them. (Deuteronomy 29:16–17)

The prophet Habakkuk contrasts such idols with the God of heaven:

> What profiteth the graven image that the maker thereof hath graven it; the molten image, and a teacher of lies, that the maker of his work trusteth therein, to make dumb idols? Woe unto him that saith to the wood, Awake; to the dumb stone, Arise, it shall teach! Behold, it is laid over with gold and silver, and there is no breath at all in the midst of it. But the LORD is in his holy temple: let all the earth keep silence before him. (Habakkuk 2:18–20)

Many Christians today believe that Satan is not a conscious, feeling being. They imagine that his mention throughout the Bible refers only to the personification of man's evil thoughts and deeds. This is a serious denial of the plain words of God in Scripture. Christ, Himself, plainly testified,

> And he [Jesus] said unto them, I beheld Satan as lightning fall from heaven. (Luke 10:18)

Clearly, Satan was once a heavenly being. The Word of God refers to him by this name no less than fifty-five times. Christ spoke of Satan by name on nineteen occasions, fifteen times in the gospels:

> Then saith Jesus unto him, Get thee hence, Satan: for it is written, Thou shalt worship the Lord thy God, and him only shalt thou serve. (Matthew 4:10)

> And if Satan cast out Satan, he is divided against himself; how shall then his kingdom stand? (Matthew 12:26)

> But he turned, and said unto Peter, Get thee behind me, Satan: thou art an offence unto me: for thou savourest not the things that be of God, but those that be of men. (Matthew 16:23)

> And he was there in the wilderness forty days, tempted of Satan; and was with the wild beasts; and the angels ministered unto him. (Mark 1:13)

> And he called them unto him, and said unto them in parables, How can Satan cast out Satan? (Mark 3:23)

> And if Satan rise up against himself, and be divided, he cannot stand, but hath an end. (Mark 3:26)

And these are they by the way side, where the word is sown; but when they have heard, Satan cometh immediately, and taketh away the word that was sown in their hearts. (Mark 4:15)

But when he had turned about and looked on his disciples, he rebuked Peter, saying, Get thee behind me, Satan: for thou savourest not the things that be of God, but the things that be of men. (Mark 8:33)

And Jesus answered and said unto him, Get thee behind me, Satan: for it is written, Thou shalt worship the Lord thy God, and him only shalt thou serve. (Luke 4:8)

And he said unto them, I beheld Satan as lightning fall from heaven. (Luke 10:18)

If Satan also be divided against himself, how shall his kingdom stand? because ye say that I cast out devils through Beelzebub. (Luke 11:18)

And ought not this woman, being a daughter of Abraham, whom Satan hath bound, lo, these eighteen years, be loosed from this bond on the sabbath day? (Luke 13:16)

Then entered Satan into Judas surnamed Iscariot, being of the number of the twelve. (Luke 22:3)

And the Lord said, Simon, Simon, behold, Satan hath desired to have you, that he may sift you as wheat. (Luke 22:31)

And after the sop Satan entered into him. Then said Jesus unto him, That thou doest, do quickly. (John 13:27)

Also Christ spoke of him in other passages of the New Testament.

> To open their eyes, and to turn them from darkness to light, and from the power of Satan unto God, that they may receive forgiveness of sins, and inheritance among them which are sanctified by faith that is in me. (Acts 26:18)

> I know thy works, and tribulation, and poverty, (but thou art rich) and I know the blasphemy of them which say they are Jews, and are not, but are the synagogue of Satan. (Revelation 2:9)

> I know thy works, and where thou dwellest, even where Satan's seat is: and thou holdest fast my name, and hast not denied my faith, even in those days wherein Antipas was my faithful martyr, who was slain among you, where Satan dwelleth. (Revelation 2:13)

> But unto you I say, and unto the rest in Thyatira, as many as have not this doctrine, and which have not known the depths of Satan, as they speak; I will put upon you none other burden. (Revelation 2:24)

> Behold, I will make them of the synagogue of Satan, which say they are Jews, and are not, but do lie; behold, I will make them to come and worship before thy feet, and to know that I have loved thee. (Revelation 3:9)

Prior to his sin Satan was known as Lucifer. The prophet Isaiah testified, under the inspiration of God, of Lucifer's sin and fall from grace:

> How art thou fallen from heaven, O Lucifer, son of the morning! how art thou cut down to the ground, which didst weaken the nations! For thou hast said in thine heart, I will ascend into heaven, I will exalt my throne above

the stars [angels] of God: I will sit also upon the mount of
the congregation, in the sides of the north: I will ascend
above the heights of the clouds [angels]; I will be like the
most High. (Isaiah 14:12–14)

What arrogance it was for a created being to dare to be classed as
equal with his Creator! No doubt if that rank had been accorded him,
which it could not have been, Lucifer would have sought to usurp the
role of God the Father, attempting to become the sole supreme ruler of
the universe. Unsanctified thirst for power knows no constraints.

So grave was Lucifer's rebellion that war erupted for the first time in
the history of the universe in its holiest center, heaven itself.

And there was war in heaven: Michael [one of Christ's
names] and his angels fought against the dragon; and the
dragon fought and his angels, and prevailed not; neither
was their place found any more in heaven. And the great
dragon was cast out, that old serpent, called the Devil,
and Satan, which deceiveth the whole world: he was cast
out into the earth, and his angels were cast out with him.
(Revelation 12:7–9)

Clearly, Satan led other angels into rebellion against the holy God
of heaven. The same chapter of Scripture identifies the proportion of
angels who were cast out of heaven. It here refers to the evil angels by
the symbol stars, a scriptural symbol for angels.

The mystery of the seven stars which thou sawest in
my right hand, and the seven golden candlesticks. The
seven stars are the angels of the seven churches: and
the seven candlesticks which thou sawest are the seven
churches. (Revelation 1:20)

And his [Satan's] tail drew the third part of the stars of
heaven, and did cast them to the earth. . . . (Revelation 12:4)

> Whereupon are the foundations thereof fastened? or who laid the corner stone thereof; when the morning stars sang together, and all the sons of God shouted for joy? (Job 38:6–7)

As we see the depth of evil prevalent in our world, the work of Satan and his fallen angels is fully revealed. The consequences of the work of Satan are fully revealed in murder, rape, immorality, pedophilia, suicide bombing and other terrorism of various kinds, mass embezzlement of funds, wars, destruction by floods, earthquakes, tornadoes, tsunamis, cyclones, droughts, deaths in the various transportation avenues of the world, marital disharmony, ingratitude of children and grandchildren, sin abounding in even professing Christian congregations, political coercion, torture, unjust laws and judicial systems and rank infidelity, materialistic idolatry and defiance of the God of heaven.

Let us now return to consider the question posed in the title of this chapter, "What if Satan were "god"? Scripture testifies that our heavenly Father is omnipotent, all powerful. He can do anything except evil. Praise God for that exception! Paul, writing to the young pastor Titus, plainly declared:

> In hope of eternal life, which God, that cannot lie, promised before the world began. (Titus 1:2)

Moses confirmed the trustworthiness of God's promises.

> God is not a man, that he should lie; neither the son of man, that he should repent: hath he said, and shall he not do it? or hath he spoken, and shall he not make it good? (Numbers 23:19)

Praise God, His Word is pure, unvarnished truth. This is our God, who is omnipotent, as the redeemed unanimously declare.

> And I heard as it were the voice of a great multitude, and as the voice of many waters, and as the voice

of mighty thunderings, saying, Alleluia: for the Lord God omnipotent reigneth. (Revelation 19:6)

And God said unto him, I am God Almighty. . . . (Genesis 35:11)

God revealed Himself to Abraham as "the Almighty God" (Genesis 17:1). In speaking of the terrible sixth plague which shall fall upon the wicked just prior to Christ's second coming, God's power is again attested.

For they are the spirits of devils, working miracles, which go forth unto the kings of the earth and of the whole world, to gather them to the battle of that great day of God Almighty. (Revelation 16:14)

Our heavenly Father is also omniscient—He knows everything, past, present and future. This is the reason that biblical prophecy is absolutely accurate in its fulfillment.

God knew every detail of us before we were even conceived.

I will praise thee; for I am fearfully and wonderfully made: marvellous are thy works; and that my soul knoweth right well. My substance was not hid from thee, when I was made in secret, and curiously wrought in the lowest parts of the earth. Thine eyes did see my substance, yet being unperfect; and in thy book all my members were written, which in continuance were fashioned, when as yet there was none of them. (Psalm 139:14–16)

How special each one of us must be to God! God had recorded every aspect of our body long before we were ever conceived. From eternity He has known our genetic make-up, our appearance, how long we would live on this earth to the very fraction of a second, and every detail of our conduct, thoughts, motives, and inclinations from conception to death.

We have often wondered which of us, being identical twins, would have been born if the single fertilized ovum from which we were formed had not divided in two. Would Colin or Russell have been born? Neither! We have lived apart since 1952, well over half a century, following our graduation from Avondale College as primary school teachers in 1951. For forty years we lived on different continents (Russell in Asia, Australia and Europe and Colin in North America). We have remained identical in our convictions and our close ties of filial love and have co-authored more than seventy books, we have ministered together in scores of nations and conducted crusades on all six inhabited continents, yet, we have absolutely no doubt that we are separate individuals. Certainly we possess no doubt of our personal identities. Had that microscopic zygote not split in our mother's womb, that individual would have possessed identical genes to us, and would have possessed our appearance. Yet the man would have possessed a different self-image from either of us, for his life's experiences would not have precisely paralleled either of ours. Indeed, he may have greatly differed from ours.

Even in one minor way, that hypothetical man had to be different in a real physical sense from one of us, for we are mirror image identical twins. Colin, born twenty minutes before Russell, is left-handed and Russell is right-handed. This fact implies that the zygote from which we formed did not split until at least ten days after conception, about which time sidedness is determined in the developing embryo. Had our zygote divided earlier we would have been either both right-handed or both left-handed. Incidentally, had the zygote split after about fourteen days, we would likely have been Siamese twins. Of course, we are very close one to the other and love one another dearly, but we assure the reader that we are thankful to God that He spared us being *that* close!

However, we each thank our Father in heaven so much that He gave each of us a living existence so that we might learn of His infinite love and the great salvation which the Godhead has offered to all men and women who genuinely believe in Him. There is so much work to do for the Lord that sometimes we wish we were identical quadruplets!

Our Father is not only omnipotent and omniscient, He is also omnipresent. Listen to the testimony of Scripture:

> For the eyes of the LORD run to and fro throughout the whole earth, to shew himself strong in the behalf of them whose heart is perfect toward him. Herein thou hast done foolishly: therefore from henceforth thou shalt have wars. (2 Chronicles 16:9)

Our loving God, speaking partially metaphorically of His necessary judgments upon the wicked, stated:

> Though they dig into hell, thence shall mine hand take them; though they climb up to heaven, thence will I bring them down: and though they hide themselves in the top of Carmel, I will search and take them out thence; and though they be hid from my sight in the bottom of the sea, thence will I command the serpent, and he shall bite them: and though they go into captivity before their enemies, thence will I command the sword, and it shall slay them: and I will set mine eyes upon them for evil, and not for good. (Amos 9:2–4)

Further, the Father is infinite:

> O the depth of the riches both of the wisdom and knowledge of God! how unsearchable are his judgments, and his ways past finding out! For who hath known the mind of the Lord? or who hath been his counsellor? Or who hath first given to him, and it shall be recompensed unto him again? For of him, and through him, and to him, are all things: to whom be glory for ever. Amen. (Romans 11:33–36)

But wonder of wonders, God is love, and He is compassionate:

> For God so loved the world, that he gave his only begotten Son, that whosoever believeth in him should not perish, but have everlasting life. (John 3:16)

> He that loveth not knoweth not God; for God is love.
> (1 John 4:8)

> And we have known and believed the love that God
> hath to us. God is love; and he that dwelleth in love dwell-
> eth in God, and God in him. (1 John 4:16)

This indisputable fact brings us back once more to the question posed in the title of this chapter—What if Satan were "god"? Let us examine some attributes of Satan. He is the arch liar. He is a mass murderer. To this Christ testified:

> Ye are of your father the devil, and the lusts of your
> father ye will do. He was a murderer from the beginning,
> and abode not in the truth, because there is no truth in
> him. When he speaketh a lie, he speaketh of his own: for
> he is a liar, and the father of it. (John 8:44)

Satan introduced war and conflict to the universe. This we have already seen. (See Revelation 12:7–9, quoted earlier in this chapter.)

The prophet Ezekiel described Satan prior to his rebellion against God, as the covering cherub, the leader of the angels, the one closest to God:

> Thou hast been in Eden the garden of God; every pre-
> cious stone was thy covering, the sardius, topaz, and the
> diamond, the beryl, the onyx, and the jasper, the sapphire,
> the emerald, and the carbuncle, and gold: the workman-
> ship of thy tabrets and of thy pipes was prepared in thee
> in the day that thou wast created. Thou art the anointed
> cherub that covereth; and I have set thee so: thou wast
> upon the holy mountain of God; thou hast walked up and
> down in the midst of the stones of fire. Thou wast perfect
> in thy ways from the day that thou wast created, till iniq-
> uity was found in thee. (Ezekiel 28:13–15)

From that high and holy station Lucifer fell and degenerated into Satan, the devil. The source of his utter rebellion against God was not kept from us, neither is the certainty of his final destruction.

> Thine heart was lifted up because of thy beauty, thou hast corrupted thy wisdom by reason of thy brightness: I will cast thee to the ground, I will lay thee before kings, that they may behold thee. Thou hast defiled thy sanctuaries by the multitude of thine iniquities, by the iniquity of thy traffick; therefore will I bring forth a fire from the midst of thee, it shall devour thee, and I will bring thee to ashes upon the earth in the sight of all them that behold thee. (Ezekiel 28:17–18)

Praise God that He is love! Imagine if Satan were "god"; that he was omnipotent, omniscient, omnipresent and infinite. Imagine if this vile, evil, hateful being could create human beings and give them life. How would this "god" of evil treat us if he possessed every infinite quality as does God, except infinite love? There is no doubt he would torture us with the most terrible agonies for eternity, preserving our lives to satisfy his sadistic glee, ever increasing the severity and pain of his treacherous acts of hate. This is no mere conjecture. Satan has injected his malevolent desire, if he possessed that power, into the Christian faith by maligning the God of heaven in attributing to Him his own vicious ambitions. Satan has convinced the majority of Christians to accept the pagan concept that the lost will be tortured in indescribable agony for eternity. (See chapter 11, "Our Father in a World of Terrorism.")

Praise our loving God that He is love! The alternative is beyond our most vivid imaginations. In his evil ambitions Lucifer had dared to envy the authority and love of the eternal God of the universe. Here was Lucifer, a mere created being, envying Deity! What presumption! Lucifer's thoughts were revealed in Scripture. We quote this fact again:

> How art thou fallen from heaven, O Lucifer, son of the morning! how art thou cut down to the ground, which

didst weaken the nations! For thou hast said in thine heart,
I will ascend into heaven, I will exalt my throne above the
stars of God: I will sit also upon the mount of the congregation, in the sides of the north: I will ascend above the
heights of the clouds; I will be like the most High. (Isaiah
14:12–14)

How grateful we are that our loving God possessed an eternal plan
to rescue us poor humans from our plight in this evil world. Those three
monosyllable words, each understood by most three-year-olds, when
joined together, form the mightiest statement testifying to God's infinite
love for us. There is no synonym in the English language for the love
expressed in the words, ***God is love***. What depth of love! What tenderness! What pity! What mercy! What grace! What compassion! What
sympathy! What kindness! What divine benevolence! What forbear-
ance! What longsuffering! In short, ***What love!*** We cry out from hearts
of gratefulness:

We love him, because he first loved us. (1 John 4:19)

Chapter 2

A Misunderstanding of the Father's Love

A GREAT number of professing Christians today possess a false understanding of the heavenly Father's tender and infinite love for us. Unknowingly they pray to the fearsome, angry, retributive deity they believe the Father to be, pleading that He will not pour out His wrath upon them with stern vengeance. Many resort to Christ's earthly mother, Mary, whom they believe is their mediatrix (female mediator) and who is the sweetest woman in the universe, pouring out her unlimited love toward us. They see Mary as their only safety from a vengeful, punitive, pitiless, primitive God, whose malignant intentions toward us sinners can only be assuaged by the intermediatory pleading of Mary.

This view has led to many placing their total faith in the one whom God chose to bear His incarnate Son. Unnumbered Christians have forgotten that our Saviour, when upon earth, taught us to address our petitions to our heavenly Father. Christ commenced the Lord's Prayer thus:

> After this manner therefore pray ye: Our Father which art in heaven, Hallowed be thy name. (Matthew 6:9)

Nowhere in Scripture are we directed to pray to God the Father through Mary. Nowhere! Numerous Christians who regularly pray the Lord's Prayer, virtually never contemplate upon our Savior's preamble to that prayer, which sets forth the Father in the glorious light of His tender, compassionate love for fallen mankind.

> Be not ye therefore like unto them: for your Father knoweth what things ye have need of, before ye ask him. (Matthew 6:8)

Here is our Father's love. He anticipates our petitions in advance. In Christ's words is an implied eagerness on the part of our heavenly Father to fulfill our every need, even anticipating each of our valid requests to Him. Listen to His loving response to our requests:

> Ask, and it shall be given you; seek, and ye shall find; knock, and it shall be opened unto you. . . . If ye then, being evil, know how to give good gifts unto your children, how much more shall your Father which is in heaven give good things to them that ask him? (Matthew 7:7, 11)

> Therefore I say unto you, What things soever ye desire, when ye pray, believe that ye receive them, and ye shall have them. (Mark 11:24)

> And whatsoever ye shall ask in my name, that will I do, that the Father may be glorified in the Son. (John 14:13)

> . . . Verily, verily, I say unto you, Whatsoever ye shall ask the Father in my name, he will give it you. Hitherto have ye asked nothing in my name: ask, and ye shall receive, that your joy may be full. (John 16:23–24)

Here we see that we should petition the Father through our Saviour. No mention is made of presenting such requests through Mary. Further, we are told in the Holy Scriptures:

> If any of you lack wisdom, let him ask of God, that giveth to all men liberally, and upbraideth not; and it shall be given him. (James 1:5)

20

> And the prayer of faith shall save the sick, and the
> Lord shall raise him up; and if he have committed sins,
> they shall be forgiven him. (James 5:15)

Our heavenly Father, who is infinite in knowledge, is too full of care for us to give us that which in His infinite wisdom He knows would harm us. The apostle Paul, writing to the Christian believers in Rome, pointed out our feebleness of mind:

> . . . we know not what we should pray for as we ought.
> . . . (Romans 8:26)

Thus God evaluates our petitions and gives us only that which He knows is best for us. He does not satisfy our selfish desires when taken before His throne, for that would only entrench sin in our hearts.

When we were little lads we recall praying to God to somehow send us a Meccano (construction) set. We well knew that in the era of the economic depression still present in the early 1940s, our parents' means did not permit such "lavish" expenditure as did that of some of our parents' more affluent friends. We are still awaiting that Meccano set. We praise God that He did answer our prayer fully, having regard to our eternal well-being. He taught us the futility of bringing before His attention our selfish wishes which would have placed within our hearts sinful motives.

Our loving heavenly Father also reminds us to come before His throne with hearts cleansed of sin, for in an old inspired Hebrew hymn He informed us:

> If I regard iniquity in my heart, the Lord will not hear
> me. (Psalm 66:18)

The only occasion when we should dare to bow before our Father's throne with unconfessed known sin in our hearts, is when we are petitioning Him to forgive us that sin and to place the power of the Holy Spirit in our hearts in order that we may live free of the repetition of that sin. Our prayer to our Father when we are convicted of sin should be akin to that of King David's after he committed adultery and connived to have the object of his lust, Bathsheba, made a widow by the slaughter of her husband, Uriah, on the battlefield at David's command.

> Have mercy upon me, O God, according to thy lov-ingkindness: according unto the multitude of thy tender mercies blot out my transgressions. Wash me throughly from mine iniquity, and cleanse me from my sin. For I acknowledge my transgressions: and my sin is ever before me. Against thee, thee only, have I sinned, and done this evil in thy sight: that thou mightest be justified when thou speakest, and be clear when thou judgest. (Psalm 51:1–4)

Today many Christians wrongfully appeal to Mary to ensure the Father answers their prayers. Others resort to various designated saints, or even to priests. Men, highly ranked in Christian circles, have made such petitions. In doing this they deny the words of Scripture—God's inspired command:

> Let us therefore come boldly unto the throne of grace, that we may obtain mercy, and find grace to help in time of need. (Hebrews 4:16)

Pope John Paul II (1921–2005; Pope 1978–2005) made this mistake when he counseled Roman Catholics to refrain from petitioning our heavenly Father for the forgiveness of our sins. Rather, he advised that absolution be requested from priests in his 1992 catechism.

We do have an intercessor with the Father, our Saviour, not because our Father is the least reluctant to pour His love upon us, but because Christ was incarnated.

> Wherefore in all things it behoved him to be made like unto his brethren, that he might be a merciful and faithful high priest in things pertaining to God, to make reconcili-ation for the sins of the people. (Hebrews 2:17)

Thus we are invited,

> For we have not an high priest which cannot be touched with the feeling of our infirmities; but was in all points tempted like as we are, yet without sin. Let us therefore come boldly unto the throne of grace, that we may obtain mercy, and find grace to help in time of need. (Hebrews 4:15–16)

Here we issue a solemn warning. Let none come presumptuously. While the members of the Godhead are, by an infinite margin, the greatest Friends we have, They are not just old mates from our neighborhood. One minister of our acquaintance recently referred to our Saviour as "mate," a common colloquialism for a human friend in Australia. He is not! In deep respect and highest reverence we must approach our God with deep humility, well aware that we are sinful creatures and He is our high and holy Creator.

But many today seek human intermediaries with God, fearing the vengeance of God. This practice extends back to antiquity among those who forsook the Father and sought to serve idols. It is a tragedy of monumental proportions that such pagan practices have found a fruitful place in Christian worship, for it is based upon a concept of God as a vicious, malicious, vindictive, and unforgiving Being. What a misrepresentation of our God of love!

Yet many sincere men and women are deluded by such sophistry. One man, Alphonsus Maria de Liguori (1696–1787), Bishop of Sant' Agata de' Goti (1762–1775), located about thirty miles (forty-eight kilometers) from Naples, Italy, who in 1732 founded the Congregation of the Most Holy Redeemer, commonly called the Redemptionists, placed a human being, Mary, in a place never accorded her in Scripture. We have the highest respect for the human mother chosen to bear Christ, but the fact must never be lost sight of that she was included in the biblical revelation that:

> For all have sinned, and come short of the glory of God. (Romans 3:23)

Bishop de Liguori was no minor prelate presiding over a minor diocese. He was an influential thinker and author. Two of his books, *The*

Glories of Mary and *The Dignity and Duties of the Priest*, have crafted thoughts and dogma far beyond his obscure See, to the point where he has received no less than three posthumous honors. Pope Gregory XVI canonized Bishop de Liguori in 1830, Pope Pius IX declared him to be a doctor of the church in 1871, thus placing the Pope's newly accorded "infallible" stamp of approval upon his writings. (The previous year, the First Vatican Council (1870) had, on December 8, voted that all popes, when making declarations *ex cathedra*, are infallible.) Further, Pope Pius XII in 1950 had declared him to be patron saint of all moralists and confessors. (See *Encyclopaedia Britannica*, 1963 edition, Vol. 14, pp. 117, 188.)

Thus Bishop St. Alphonsus de Liguori wrote with a pen of authority and may be quoted as a standard of truth for about two-thirds of all professing Christians today. He wrote:

> Whereas it is said of other saints that they are with God, of Mary alone can it be affirmed that not only is she subject to the will of God, but God is subject to her will. (de Liguori, *Glories of Mary*, Benziger Brothers, New York, 1902, p. 43)

> The Roman Church applies to her [Mary] the following words: He that shall find me shall find life, and shall have salvation from the Lord. (Ibid.)

> The whole salvation of the world lies in the abundance of the favor of Mary. (Ibid.)

> Many things are asked from God and are not granted. They are asked from Mary and are obtained. (Ibid.)

> Mary is our only refuge, help and asylum. (Ibid.)

Further, Antonio Perozzi (1389–1459), Archbishop of Florence (1446–1469), canonized 1523, known in Roman Catholic circles as St. Antoninus, claimed in his book *Summa moralis*, that, whoever asks and expects to obtain graces without the intercession of Mary endeavors to fly without wings.

Again we emphasize that Mary was a human of high virtue, but she required the death and resurrection of the One she was privileged above all women to bear and to Whom she gave birth in His incarnate state. To raise her to the status of a goddess, is to take Christians back to rank paganism which fears the god of wrath and vengeance. Many Christians today do not recognize that the deification of this lovely human being does her memory no justice and denigrates our Father of love.

Walter Woodburn Hyde (born 1870), professor of Greek, Latin and ancient history in several American universities, rightly commented:

> It is not difficult, then, to understand why the Romans, at first repelled by the strange rites of Isis [the Egyptian mother goddess], were later attracted by them; the ordinary woman, by the splendid processions and the novelty of what she saw; the educated, by the antiquity and impressiveness of the ritual, the beautiful drama, the tenderness of Isis, her rigorous rules of abstinence and purification, communion with deity, separation of her clergy from the world, and especially the final judgment and promise of a blissful hereafter with her, here emphasized more than in any other of her sister religions. She, as the "universal woman" and "queen of heaven" also attracted men as well as women. Her ritual bore a marked resemblance to that of early Christianity, as Sir James Frazer has pointed out:
> "Indeed the stately ritual with its shaven and tonsured priests, its matins and vespers, its tinkling music, its baptisms as aspersions of holy water, its solemn processions, its jeweled images of the mother of God, presented many points of similarity to the pomp and ceremonies of Catholicism." [Note 36: *Adonis, Attis and Osiris* (2nd ed.; London), p. 347]

25

Isis was, then, the *mater dolorosa* of paganism who sympathized especially with mothers in their sorrows and afflictions. In his prayer Lucius [Apuleius] says: "[Thou] by thy bounty and grace nourishest all the world, and bearest a great affection to the adversities of the miserable as a loving mother. . . . Thou art she that puttest away all storms and dangers from men's life by stretching forth thy right hand. . .and appeasest the great tempests of fortune. . . ." (Dr. Walter Hyde, *Paganism to Christianity in the Roman Empire*, University of Pennsylvania Press, Philadelphia, 1946, p. 54)

With the conversion of Emperor Constantine to Christianity in the early fourth century, a huge number of European and North African pagans embraced his example. Initially this appeared to be the culmination of Christ's command for Christian evangelism, in the eyes of undiscerning Christians.

Go ye therefore, and teach all nations, baptizing them in the name of the Father, and of the Son, and of the Holy Ghost: teaching them to observe all things whatsoever I have commanded you: and, lo, I am with you alway, even unto the end of the world. Amen. (Matthew 28:19–20)

But ye shall receive power, after that the Holy Ghost is come upon you: and ye shall be witnesses unto me both in Jerusalem, and in all Judaea, and in Samaria, and unto the uttermost part of the earth. (Acts 1:8)

And he said unto them, Go ye into all the world, and preach the gospel to every creature. (Mark 16:15)

It was during the era of Constantine's "conversion" that, very slowly initially, but later with growing momentum, Jesus' mother, Mary, gained divine attributes in the hearts and minds of many Christians.

It is, then, only natural that some students have seen her [the Egyptian goddess, Isis'] influence as "mother of sorrows" and "mother of Horus," in whom the Greeks saw their grief-stricken Demeter searching for her daughter Persephone raped by Pluto, on the Christian concept of Mary. The motif of mother and child appears in many statuettes which have been found in her ruined shrines on the Seine, Rhine, and Danube, and which the early Christians mistook for the Madonna and Child, and little wonder since it is still difficult to differentiate between the two types.

The epithet "Mother of God" (*Theotokos*) as applied to Mary seems to have been used at first by Alexandrian theologians at the close of the third century, although it does not appear in any extant writing of that period. It became common in the fourth, being used by Eusebius, Athanasius, Gregory of Nazianzus in Cappadocia and others, Gregory saying that "the man who does not believe Mary was the *Theotokos* has no part in God." (Dr. Walter Hyde, *op. cit.,* p. 54)

Dr. Gordon Jennings Laing (1869–1945) offered other insights into the insinuation of the concept of Mary with attributes accorded her, into the Christian faith. Dr. Laing, a Canadian who was a professor of Latin and Dean of the Faculty of Arts, McGill University, Canada, and later Dean of Humanities at the University of Chicago, made an extensive examination of the historical facts concerning a Phrygian pagan goddess, Cybele, whose supposed qualities and titles later became merged into the deification of Mary.

The cult of this Phrygian divinity, variously called the Mother of the Gods, Cybele, the Great Mother or the Idaean Mother, was introduced into Rome in 204 BC. . . . Although this cult was one of the last to yield to Christianity and persisted obstinately after most of the other pagan forms of worship had passed away, it left but few traces of its protracted dominance. To be sure, points of contact with the Virgin Mary have been pointed out. One of Mary's titles, "the Mother of God" (Gran Madre di Dio), has inevitable reminiscences of the pagan "Mother of the Gods." Moreover, many a visitor to Rome and student of sculpture has commented on the resemblance between the statues of the two. Furthermore, we know that the shrine of the Virgin on Monte Vergine near Avellino in the Apennines not far from Naples, which is visited each year by thousands of pilgrims, attracted by the fame of the wonder-working image there, was once the site of the temple of the Great Mother. That they were confused in people's minds is shown by the question which an unbeliever addressed to Abbot Isidore of Pelusium in the sixth century. He asked what the difference was between the Magna Mater of the pagans and the Magna Mater Maria of the Christians. But mother-goddesses, whatever their origin or special characteristics, are bound to have certain features in common. Nor is there much reason for surprise in finding in Claudia's prayer to the Great Mother a tone analogous to that of any prayer to the sanctissima Maria in modern times: "Hear my prayer, thou who art the gentle mother of the gods." . . . (Dr. Gordon Laing, *Survivals of Roman Religions*, Longmans, New York, 1931, pp. 122–124)

The Phrygian nation developed in the northwest and central region of present-day Turkey, somewhere between 1500 and 1200 BC, and this nation eventually fell under the dominion of other races, including the Celts of the biblical province of Galatia, finally disappearing from history about 300 AD. The Phrygians spoke an Indo-European language. In a sense, the expiry of the Phrygian civilization occurred at that time as a result of Emperor Constantine's professed conversion to the faith of Jesus. Tragically, after the extinction of the Phrygian civilization, elements of their pagan religion survived as it became merged into the formerly pure Christian faith. Mary was elevated by Christians from a godly woman to a human who became a goddess. This paganization of Christ's elevated faith persists to our day.

The best known cleric of the late twentieth and early twenty-first century, Pope John Paul II (Pope 1978–2005) held Mary not simply as a very virtuous human being, but far beyond to the status as co-mediatrix and co-redeemer with our Saviour.

Scripture, the source of all truth, stands in stony silence on these claims. Read the Bible countless times, and these matters will not be found, nor does Scripture ever allude to them. We must never forget that these highly exaggerated and totally extra-scriptural claims of our Savior's wonderful earthly mother have grown out of the pagan fear of our heavenly Father. Many Christians had been deluded by Satan's misrepresentation of God as a fierce, angry being, burning with rage and thirsting for vengeance against sinners.

How different is the Bible-based evaluation of each of the three members of the Godhead provided by the finest biblical expositor of the nineteenth and twentieth centuries, Ellen Gould (Harmon) White (1827–1915). Looking at the fearful moment in history of this planet when Adam and Eve introduced sin into the human race, this expositor perceptively wrote:

> The Godhead was stirred with pity for the race, and the Father, the Son, and the Holy Spirit gave Themselves to the working out of the plan of redemption. In order fully to carry out this plan, it was decided that Christ, the only-begotten Son of God, should give Himself an offering for sin. What line can measure the depth of this love? God would make it impossible for man to say that He could have done more. With Christ He gave all the resources of heaven, that nothing might be wanting in the plan for man's uplifting. Here is love—the contemplation of which should fill the soul with inexpressible gratitude! Oh, what love, what matchless love! The contemplation of this love

will cleanse the soul from all selfishness. It will lead the disciple to deny self, take up the cross, and follow the Redeemer. (*Counsels on Health*, p. 222–223)

The writer was an American, but she spent two years in Europe (1884–1886) and nine years (1891–1900) in Australia. Surely this brief statement fully testified to the tender love and pity of our heavenly Father as so clearly enunciated in Scripture.

But God commendeth his love toward us, in that, while
we were yet sinners, Christ died for us. (Romans 5:8)

Instead of annihilating our first parents for their inexcusable rebellion against Him, our Father sat down in pity, not wrath, not revenge, but rather in a redemptive spirit full of love, to rescue mankind from eternal destruction and to restore them to Eden once more. That is the God of love who calls each of us today to His glorious kingdom. The authors find such love irresistible.

CHAPTER 3

Our Loving Father and Mary

ONE may search the Scriptures from cover to cover, yet discover not the least inkling that Mary, the mother of Jesus, possessed a single characteristic of deity. If Mary was indeed a co-mediatrix or a co-redemptrix, this would prove the Bible to be a book of faulted information, depriving human beings of crucial information essential for their salvation.

Such an implied view of Scripture would denigrate the numerous words of its pages, which promise that

> When he, the Spirit of truth, is come, he will guide you into *all truth*. . . . (John 16:13)

Through the prophet Isaiah, God made a solemn promise to mankind which, even if this was the lone such Bible promise, would totally preclude Mary as the avenue to salvation. Christ alone died for our salvation:

> He was oppressed, and he was afflicted, yet he opened not his mouth: he is brought as a lamb to the slaughter, and as a sheep before her shearers is dumb, so he openeth not his mouth. He was taken from prison and from judgment: and who shall declare his generation? for he was cut off out of the land of the living: for the transgression of my people was he stricken. (Isaiah 53:7–8)

Yet, Australia's most respected news weekly, *The Bulletin*, reported in its issue of September 2, 1997, that

The Catholic Church in Australia is preparing to grapple with a worldwide push among many church members to elevate the Virgin Mary to co-redeemer status with Jesus.

Newsweek, August 25, 1997 reported:

A growing movement in the Roman Catholic Church wants the pope to proclaim a new, controversial dogma: that Mary is a Co-Redeemer.

The article went on to record that

This week a large box shipped from California and addressed to, "His Holiness, John Paul II" will arrive at the Vatican. The shipping label lists a dozen countries—from every continent but Antarctica—plus a number, 40,383, indicating the quantity of signatures inside. Each signature is attached to a petition asking the pope to exercise the power of infallibility to proclaim a new dogma of the Roman Catholic faith that the Virgin Mary is "Co-Redemptrix, Mediatrix of All Graces and Advocate for the people of God." (Ibid.)

Who is our Redeemer?

As for our redeemer, the LORD of hosts is his name, the Holy One of Israel. (Isaiah 47:4)

Thus saith the LORD, thy Redeemer, the Holy One of Israel; I am the LORD thy God which teacheth thee to profit, which leadeth thee by the way that thou shouldest go. (Isaiah 48:17)

Doubtless thou art our father, though Abraham be ignorant of us, and Israel acknowledge us not: thou, O LORD, art our father, our redeemer; thy name is from everlasting. (Isaiah 63:16)

And I will feed them that oppress thee with their own flesh; and they shall be drunken with their own blood, as with sweet wine: and all flesh shall know that I the LORD am thy Saviour and thy Redeemer, the mighty One of Jacob. (Isaiah 49:26)

See also Isaiah 43:14; 44:6, 24; 49:7; 54:5, 6; 60:16.

Who is our Mediator?

For there is one God, and one mediator between God and men, the man Christ Jesus. (1 Timothy 2:5)

Who is our Advocate?

My little children, these things write I unto you, that ye sin not. And if any man sin, we have an advocate with the Father, Jesus Christ the righteous. (1 John 2:1)

Who are our Intercessors?

Therefore will I divide him a portion with the great, and he shall divide the spoil with the strong; because he hath poured out his soul unto death: and he was numbered with the transgressors; and he bare the sin of many, and made intercession for the transgressors. (Isaiah 53:12)

Likewise the Spirit also helpeth our infirmities: for we know not what we should pray for as we ought: but the Spirit [Christ's representative] itself maketh intercession for us with groanings which cannot be uttered. And he that searcheth the hearts knoweth what is the mind of the Spirit, because he maketh intercession for the saints according to the will of God. (Romans 8:26–27)

Who is he that condemneth? It is Christ that died, yea rather, that is risen again, who is even at the right hand of God, who also maketh intercession for us. (Romans 8:34)

Wherefore he is able also to save them to the uttermost that come unto God by him, seeing he [Jesus] ever liveth to make intercession for them. (Hebrews 7:25)

What a blasphemous disgrace for men and women to think that they can wrest from our Saviour His sole rights as our Redeemer, Mediator, Advocate, and Intercessor! What disdain of Scripture! What blindness and folly!

The *Newsweek* article reported that 4,340,429 signatures supporting this gross absurdity had been received from 157 countries. Nor were the proposers of this preposterous dogma confined to non-entities in the Roman Catholic Church.

Among the notable supporters are Mother Teresa of Calcutta, nearly 500 bishops and 42 cardinals, including John O'Connor of New York, Joseph Glemp of Poland and half a dozen cardinals at the Vatican itself. (Ibid.)

As the implications of such dogma are spelled out, the challenge to Christ by the papal antichrist power is clearly discerned:

If this drive succeeds, Catholics would be obliged as a matter of faith to accept three extraordinary doctrines: that Mary participated in the redemption along with her son, that all graces that flow from the suffering and death of Jesus Christ are granted only through Mary's intercession with her son and that all prayers and petitions from the faithful on earth must likewise flow through Mary, who then brings them to the attention of Jesus. (Ibid.)

Words alone cannot describe this destruction of biblical teaching. Mary was a godly woman, but, like ourselves, she was a sinner, requiring the redemption which her Saviour, Jesus Christ, bought for mankind on Calvary and bestows through His high-priestly ministry in the heavenly sanctuary. Mary shed no blood for the salvation of the human race. Yet Scripture plainly states,

> And almost all things are by the law purged with blood; and without shedding of blood is no remission. (Hebrews 9:22)

Mary did not lead a perfect life as Jesus did. Mary is not our ministering heavenly high priest. Christ, alone is our heavenly High Priest.

> Seeing then that we have a great high priest, that is passed into the heavens, Jesus the Son of God, let us hold fast our profession. (Hebrews 4:14)

> But this man, because he [Jesus] continueth ever, hath an unchangeable priesthood. Wherefore he is able also to save them to the uttermost that come unto God by him, seeing he ever liveth to make intercession for them. For such an high priest became us, who is holy, harmless, undefiled, separate from sinners, and made higher than the heavens. (Hebrews 7:24–26)

To even suggest that Mary plays a part in our redemption is to belittle our redemption and place it, at least partially, in the hands of a mere human, a status which not even the godliest human who has ever trod this earth merits. To substitute a sinner to do the work in place of our eternal Redeemer, "the mighty God, the everlasting Father" (Isaiah 9:6) is a concept so outrageous, so alien to the words of Holy Writ, such a depth of blasphemy, that no devout Christian should ever countenance it for a fraction of a second. Only the arch-deceiver could place such musings in the minds of human beings.

As *Newsweek* commented in the mildest of terms,

> This is what theologians call high Mariology, and it seems to contradict the basic New-Testament belief that "there is one God and one mediator between God and man, Christ Jesus." (1 Timothy 2:5) In place of the Holy Trinity, it would appear, there would be a kind of Holy Quartet, with Mary playing the multiple roles of daughter of the Father, mother of the Son and spouse of the Holy Spirit. (Ibid.)

Alarming is the fact that Pope John Paul II, at the date of the article had

> referred to her [Mary] as Co-Redemptrix' at least five times. (Ibid.)

In April 1977, John Paul II declared,

> Having created man "male and female," the Lord also wants to place the New Eve [Mary] beside the New Adam [Christ] in the Redemption. . . . Mary, the New Eve, thus becomes a perfect icon of the Church. . . . We can therefore turn to the Blessed Virgin, trustfully imploring her aid in awareness of the singular role entrusted to her by God, the role of co-operator in the Redemption. (Quoted in Ibid.)

Since John Paul II attributed to Mary the sparing of his life during an assassination attempt in 1981, he was motivated to spare her no accolade, no elevation of status. But since Mary is dead, she could have played no part in the sparing of the Pope's life, for

> . . . the dead know not any thing. . . . (Ecclesiastes
> 9:5)

(See our book *Mystery of Death* and also the chapter entitled "Death" in the seventh book of the Antichrist Septenate—*The Rapture, The End Times and the Millennium.*)

It is likely that political considerations were the sole reason which restrained the Pope from declaring Mary's supposed role in human redemption to be official Roman Catholic Church dogma. At a time when the Roman Catholic Church was increasing its influence in Protestant churches, the Pope may have deemed that the proclamation of the status of Mary as our co-redemptrix would have caused consternation in many of the churches of Protestantism, thus imperiling some of the gains it had made. In fact, this church has for centuries ascribed to Mary almost all attributes of redemption except that of having died on the cross of Calvary. These have been accepted, despite the fact that Mary was a sinner, herself, in need of redemption.

> For ***all*** have sinned, and come short of the glory of
> God. (Romans 3:23)

Further, Pope Pius IX's December 8, 1854, declaration of the Dogma of the Immaculate Conception of Mary added support to the exaggerated and blasphemous papal claims concerning Mary. Again, we emphasize that Mary was a wonderful woman, chosen of God for the most sacred role ever accorded a woman, the motherhood of the world's Redeemer. But to go beyond this is to destroy the entire plan of redemption and to place in the hands of a woman, one who herself required a redeemer, the rights of Christ alone in the work of our redemption. In the Old-Testament sacrificial types and ceremonies, Christ was prefigured in all as our Sacrifice for sin and as our ministering High Priest. There is not the slightest hint that Mary or any human participated in our salvation. In denial of the scriptural assertion that every human being has sinned (see Romans 3:23 above), Catholicism makes a falsehood of God's Word by declaring that Mary was without the smallest actual sin throughout the whole course of her life. . . . No breath of sin ever sullied the purity of her soul. She was not only without sin, original or actual, but she was also in a certain sense incapable of sinning because of a special privilege. ("Impeccability and Pre-destination of Mary," *The Sign*, The Passionist Missions Inc., Union City, New Jersey, August 1941, p. 48)

The same tract went on to assert that Mary's

preservation from original sin also included her preservation from concupiscence, that disorderly affection in the human soul that inclines men to sin, though it is not sin itself. (Ibid.)

Of course, Mary bore no original sin. This is yet another false doctrine, based not upon Scripture, but false tradition. Many Protestants who espouse the doctrine of original sin are quite unaware of the nature of that doctrine. It is defined below:

Adam lost original justice, not only for himself but also for us; that he poured sin, which is the death of the soul, into the human race and that sin comes, not by imitation of Adam's transgression, but by propagation from him. (Addis and Arnold, *The Catholic Dictionary*, 1884)

Peter de Rosa, retired Roman Catholic Professor and priest, expressed the doctrine of original sin in even sterner terms. Speaking of the views of Pope Gregory I (the Great) (Pope 590–604), de Rosa wrote,

Day-old babies born of Christian parents went to hell if they died unbaptized. (*Vicars of Christ*, Corgi Books, England, 1989, p. 460)

De Rosa quoted Dr. William Edward Hartpole Lecky (1838–1903), member of the British House of Commons, Irish historian and essayist, who placed the matter in its most repugnant form:

> That a little child who lives but a few minutes after birth and dies before it has been sprinkled with the sacred water is in such a sense responsible for its ancestor [Adam] having six thousand years before eaten a forbidden fruit . . . may with perfect justice be resuscitated and cast into an abyss of eternal fire in expiation of this ancestral crime, that an all-righteous and merciful Creator, in the full exercise of these attributes, deliberately calls into existence sentient beings whom He had from eternity irrevocably destined to endure unspeakable, unmitigated torture, are propositions which are at once so extravagantly absurd and so ineffably atrocious that their adoption might lead men to doubt the universality of moral perception. Such teaching is, in fact, simply demonism, and demonism in its most extreme form. (*Ibid*, p. 461)

This false view of original sin sets God forth as a vengeful monster, condemning men unacquainted, through no fault of their own, to eternal damnation.

> Francis Xavier went to the Indies . . . certain that unbaptized pagans, *however virtuous*, could not get to heaven. (*Ibid*, p. 460)

The Bible declares otherwise:

> For as many as have sinned without law shall also perish without law: and as many as have sinned in the law shall be judged by the law; (For not the hearers of the law are just before God, but the doers of the law shall be justified. For when the Gentiles, which have not the law,

do by nature the things contained in the law, these, having not the law, are a law unto themselves: which shew the work of the law written in their hearts, their conscience also bearing witness, and their thoughts the mean while accusing or else excusing one another;) in the day when God shall judge the secrets of men by Jesus Christ according to my gospel. (Romans 2:12–16)

In God's mercy, pagans will be judged by the minimal light which they have known. They will be ignorant of Christ, but in the kingdom of heaven, He will sit with them and gently explain their salvation. The Scripture tenderly depicts this scene.

And one shall say unto him, What are these wounds in thine hands? Then he shall answer, Those with which I was wounded in the house of my friends. (Zechariah 13:6)

We are not sinners because we are conceived; we are sinners because, like Adam, we have all transgressed God's law.

We quote the words of Dr. Gordon J. Laing. In his book, *Survivals of Roman Religion*, he illustrates the perceived usefulness of accepting the pagan concepts of the Saxons and introducing them into Christian thought by none other than a canonized Pope.

The idea of [the Egyptian goddess] Isis as the mother of the child Horus was in many minds transferred to Mary, mother of God. "Remember," said Gregory the Great [Pope St. Gregory I], when issuing his instructions to a missionary to the Saxon heathens, "that you must not interfere with any traditional belief or religious observance that can be harmonized with Christianity." And the policy of the Church toward the Saxons was not unique. The same method was used in dealing with pagans everywhere. It was the bridge over which untold thousands passed from paganism to the new faith. Without this adaptability Christianity might not have succeeded. The shift from Isis to Mary was one of the easiest and most obvious. There are extant statuettes and figurines of Isis nursing Horus which are marked by a striking similarity to familiar representations of the Madonna and Child. It is said that sometimes images of this kind have been mistaken for representations of Mary and Jesus and have actually been worshipped in Christian Churches. . . . (*Survivals of Roman Religion*, Dr. Gordon J. Laing, p. 129, first square brackets in original)

We would seriously question Dr. Laing's assertion that without absorbing pagan concepts "Christianity might not have succeeded." In this his judgment was poor. In fact, if it had been presented in its purity, Christianity would long before now have enlightened the whole world. When we add pagan thought to the Christian faith it is paganism which flourishes while Christianity and our loving God are debased.

CHAPTER 4

Our Loving Father and Eternal Torment

THE devil gods of paganism have ever been portrayed as demons who would delight in the fearful torture of poor humans indefinitely, obtaining diabolical glee from their unending agonies and unceasing screams for mercy. But there is no mercy. Pagans feared these devil gods, believing that there was no relief from the most terrible suffering which the demons heartlessly and in great satisfaction relentlessly imposed.

In pagan Buddhism today, the concept of torture after death is embedded in this faith, accepted by millions of adherents in Sri Lanka, Tibet, China, India, Burma, Japan, Thailand, Cambodia, Laos, Malaysia and Singapore. Yet this is the religion to which many in the Western world have become attracted. Oh, if only Christians had proclaimed and had reflected the love of God in their lives many of these searching souls would be embracing the God of the universe. How we have betrayed our Saviour and God!

The view of Buddhism, as modified by the Chinese culture, is a little different from Buddhism in some other cultures. While Chinese Buddhists believe in reincarnation, they also believe that the soul endures unspeakable tortures between incarnations in order to cleanse it from sin. Of course, the greater the sins the worse the torment.

This view is well illustrated in the Tiger Balm Gardens in Singapore. There a series of most terrible tortures are illustrated in sculptured models. These include disemboweled individuals having their bowels fried while still attached to the body, legs being ground in a grinding machine and spears piercing the eyes. There are many more forms of tortures which are designed in an attempt to terrify individuals into lives of holiness.

The Thai Buddhists have a more subtle view of hell. It has been asserted that an individual who dies a sinner will suffer unspecified terrible punishment for a period of one Kappa. This is not a time period even used normally in Thailand. However this period has been described in an imaginative way. There is a mountain ten miles high (twice the height of Mount Everest) and forty miles in circumference. Once every one hundred years a celestial being comes from heaven and wipes the mountain with a cloth as soft as a cloud. When, after myriads of such wipings, the mountain is leveled to the height of the surrounding countryside, then the era of one Kappa is completed! Thus is eternal hell described.

Only a devilish fiend could imagine such fearful atrocities, and Satan is such a fiend. If he were the uninhibited ruler of the world, he would delight in such deeds. By contrast the fearful tortures perpetrated in Abu Ghraib and Guantanamo Bay would seem like heavenly bliss. In contrast, we serve a God who is love. (See 1 John 4:8)

Russell served as a physician in Southeast Asia for a total of two decades. In this period he lived ten years in Malaysia, six and a half years in Thailand, and three years in Singapore, as well as visiting other countries where Buddhism is revered by many, including Brunei, Burma, Cambodia, China, India, Japan, Laos, Sri Lanka, Taiwan, and Vietnam.

Among the Chinese of Malaysia, Russell was amazed to observe many Buddhist practices akin to Roman Catholicism as largely practiced today, in the absence of any mandate from Scripture. We cite a few of these. Buddhists in Malaysia wear a cross, albeit the broken cross of the swastika, around their necks to symbolize their faith. They possess designated human saints whom they depict with a halo about their heads. The Buddhists hold processions on an annual basis, four men carrying upon their shoulders an idol of the Goddess of Mercy encased in glass. Professed Christians perform an almost identical rite, carrying an image of Our Lady of Fatima on their shoulders. Likewise, the Buddhists designate certain days for abstinence from the eating of meat. Both religions possess an annual Lent of forty days, where the ingestion of meat is forbidden.

Both religious groups pray for their deceased ancestors at a designated time of the year, the Buddhists during the Feast of the Hungry Ghosts and the Catholics on All Souls' Day. Both use prayer beads, known among the

Catholics as rosary beads. Each possess clergy, both male and female, who must remain celibate—the priests, monks and nuns of Catholicism and the monks and nuns of Buddhism. Both prescribe for monks the shaving of the head. No biblical injunction for these "Christian" duties exists.

The parallels between Buddhism and the majority of professed Christians today, which extend to the concept of the immortality of the soul, are no coincidence. Such practices originated in a common source—the paganism of North Africa and the Middle East. Almost imperceptibly, yet all too rapidly, from its early days, the Christian church embraced pagan practices. The first center for this rank apostasy was the city of Alexandria in Egypt, the greatest focus of Greek learning. Early Christians, beguiled by the reputation of Alexandria as the pinnacle of Greek civilization, early imbibed pagan principles, applying them to Christian thought. Clement of Alexandria (c. AD 150–215) led out in this perversion of the pure Christian faith. His full name was Titus Flavius Clemens. The dates ascribed to his life are close approximations.

However, so strong was the prestige and influence of the Greek philosophers in that region of the world that, before Clement, other early second-century leaders, including Justin Martyr (c. 114–165) and Tatian (died c. 180), also had sought to understand Christianity through the filter of Greek paganism.

Clement was a

> Christian presbyter, whose writings mark an epoch in early Christian intellectual development; [he was] born of pagan parents, probably in Athens. (*Encyclopaedia Britannica*, 1963 edition, Vol. 5, p. 899)

Thinking he was enhancing the intellectual reputation of Christianity among the Greek pagan intelligentsia, St. Clement (as Roman Catholics address him) merged Greek philosophy with biblical truths. Such a faulted approach shamed our loving God and set in progress a destruction of Christian faith which had despoiled it progressively as the centuries of the Christian era have rolled by, until today we see the vilest practices openly endorsed.

Clement was the intellectual leader of the Alexandrian Christian community: he wrote several ethical and theological works and biblical commentaries; he combated heretical Gnostics (religious dualists who believed in salvation through esoteric knowledge that revealed to men their spiritual origins, identities, and destinies); he engaged in polemics with Christians who were suspicious of an intellectualized Christianity; and he educated persons who later became theological and ecclesiastical leaders (*e.g.,* Alexander, bishop of Jerusalem). (*Ibid,* 2000 CD Edition)

Here we see that Clement's influence and his false pagan teachings spread widely. Clement equated the Mosaic law, written by God's own finger, with the pagan Greek philosophy.

Clement presented a functional program of witnessing in thought and action to Hellenistic inquirers and Christian believers, a program that he hoped would bring about an understanding of the role of Greek philosophy and the Mosaic tradition within the Christian faith. According to Clement, philosophy was to the Greeks as the Law of Moses was to the Jews, a preparatory discipline leading to the truth, which was personified in the *Logos*. His goal was to make Christian beliefs intelligible to those trained within the context of the Greek *paideia* [educational curriculum] so that those who accepted the Christian faith might be able to witness effectively within Hellenistic culture. He also was a social critic deeply rooted in the 2nd-century cultural milieu. (Ibid.)

Clement's view, "One, therefore, is the way of truth, but into it, just as into an everlasting river, flow streams but from another place" (*Stromateis*), prepared the way for the curriculum of the catechetical school under Origen [c. 184–254] that became the basis of the medieval quadrivium and trivium (*i.e.,* the liberal arts). This view, however, did not find ready acceptance by the uneducated orthodox Christians of Alexandria, who looked askance at intellectuals. (Ibid.)

Thus we see a major avenue through which Christianity became polluted by Pagan concepts in the second century of its existence. Yet, as always, there were humble, devout Christians who resisted the paganization of the pure faith of God. One of the most prominent heroes of active opposition to the Hellenizing of Christianity was Lucian of Antioch in Syria (c. 250–312) who was finally martyred. He stood courageously against the pagan infiltration of the Alexandrian school of Clement and Origen though he lived subsequent to their sad histories. He and his pupils also scribed hundreds of New-Testament Greek manuscripts free from the alterations made by the Alexandrian school of theology.

Those standing nobly for God's truth, as so often occurs, were not men and women of worldly eminence, but true believers, filled with the love of God and His Word. The same class of individuals followed the Son of God.

> . . . And the common people heard him [Jesus] gladly.
> (Mark 12:37)

The ordaining of openly homosexual clerics, including the Episcopalian Bishop of New Hampshire in 2004, and the endorsement of such defilers of the faith as ministers of the Uniting Church of Australia in 2005 (this church is a combination of Congregationalists, Methodists and Presbyterians), present two of many examples. Immorality of every kind including adultery, pedophilia, pornography, and even incest is found in most, if not all, Christian Churches, all of which claim to be worshipers of our heavenly Father. Many churches offer sports and other forms of entertainment, rather than God and His salvation truths. Outrageous rock music and forms of vaudeville pervade many churches as worship, as if our Father in heaven is a wild, maniacal deity of demonic character.

46

Scripture is precise in its requirements in respect of our worship of a pure, holy and awesome loving Father.

> Give unto the LORD the glory due unto his name: bring an offering, and come before him: worship the LORD in the beauty of holiness. (1 Chronicles 16:29)

When angels who have never defiled themselves through sin enter the presence of the Father, their awe, reverence and respect know no bounds. Isaiah was privileged to witness such sacred adoration.

> In the year that king Uzziah died I saw also the Lord sitting upon a throne, high and lifted up, and his train filled the temple. Above it stood the seraphims: each one had six wings; with twain he covered his face, and with twain he covered his feet, and with twain he did fly. And one cried unto another, and said, Holy, holy, holy, is the LORD of hosts: the whole earth is full of his glory. (Isaiah 6:1–3)

Yet we pathetic mortals defile and pollute our worship services, casting God's presence from our midst and inviting Satan and his evil host in.

It is time that those who profess to love the Infinite God remember that He has declared:

> I dwell in the high and holy place, with him also that is of a contrite and humble spirit, to revive the spirit of the humble, and to revive the heart of the contrite ones. (Isaiah 57:15)

In line with the utter despoiling of our Father's name and character is the abominable pagan concept of an ever-burning hell. This pagan fiction is documented in chapter five.

CHAPTER 5

The Pagan Roots of a Vengeful Heavenly Father

A LARGE group of Christians postulate that our heavenly Father is described in Scripture as a God who burns a soul lost in sin for eternity. But surely this strikes a discordant chord in the mind of all rational beings. In a verse added by John Rees about 1889 to John Newton's (1725–1807) much-loved hymn, Amazing Grace, he correctly states:

> When we've been there ten thousand years,
> Bright shining as the sun,
> We've no less days, to sing God's praise
> Than when we'd first begun.

Here in poetic words, is encapsulated the glorious fact that God's faithful people will exist for an infinity of time in great bliss. This is true to Scripture.

> And I saw a new heaven and a new earth: for the first heaven and the first earth were passed away; and there was no more sea. And I John saw the holy city, new Jerusalem, coming down from God out of heaven, prepared as a bride adorned for her husband. And I heard a great voice out of heaven saying, Behold, the tabernacle of God is with men, and he will dwell with them, and they shall be his people, and God himself shall be

with them, and be their God. And God shall wipe away all tears from their eyes; and there shall be no more death, neither sorrow, nor crying, neither shall there be any more pain: for the former things are passed away. (Revelation 21:1–4)

Here is a plain promise from our God, who cannot lie (Titus 1:2), that God's redeemed will never die.

If we believed that the lost will live eternally in the most indescribable agony, in revenge for a mere seventy years of sin, it would paint God as a fiend for devising the most disproportionate punishments possibly conceived in any mind. Our God would be a hellish demon. Such a concept has turned millions of reasoning minds to a perceived fortress of unreasoning infidelity. Sadly through the hundreds of years of the dark and middle ages, when illiteracy was the lot of the majority of the population of Europeans, there was no way for Christians to examine Scripture to determine the error of this doctrine. Worse still, added to the illiterate, were those non-clerical literates who were forbidden to study Holy Scripture on pain of death. It was claimed that the priests also were prepared to discern the beliefs of the Bible.

John Rees' words concerning the redeemed, could be perverted, less poetically, to apply to those bearing such punishment, to read:

> When they've been there ten trillion years
> In fearful agony,
> They've no less days to suffer on
> Than when they first begun.

But praise God, He loves the sinner! The Godhead's infinite rescue plan for sinners proclaims this fact in deafening tones which soften our hard hearts. Our Father spared nothing in order to provide salvation for all who would accept it. One would conclude that such a prospect, with not a single drawback, bearing no imperfection, would be grasped eagerly by all mankind. But Scripture testifies otherwise. Quoting Isaiah 10:22, 34 and 1:9, Paul declared otherwise when applying these ancient prophecies to the last generation alive on this earth at the time of Christ's second advent:

> Esaias [the Greek name for the Hebrew prophet Isaiah] also crieth concerning Israel, Though the number of the children of Israel be as the sand of the sea, a remnant shall be saved: for he will finish the work, and cut it short in righteousness: because a short work will the Lord make upon the earth. And as Esaias said before, Except the Lord of Sabaoth had left us a seed, we had been as Sodoma, and been made like unto Gomorrha. (Romans 9:27–29)

Paul referred here, not to the entire world population, but to professing Christians only. Using the term "Israel," a biblical term for the professed followers of Christ, he foretold that only a remnant would be saved. In fact the passage to which he alluded from Isaiah's end-time prophecy was even more telling.

> Except the LORD of hosts had left unto us a very small remnant, we should have been as Sodom, and we should have been like unto Gomorrah. (Isaiah 1:9)

A "remnant" indicates a small proportion of an item or group. A "small remnant" is, of course, smaller still, while "a very small remnant" shrinks the numbers even more significantly. Is this, then, a cause for despair? Certainly not! God has promised, speaking of His offered call to salvation registered in the final chapter of the Bible,

> And the Spirit and the bride say, Come. And let him that heareth say, Come. And let him that is athirst come. And whosoever will, let him take the water of life freely. (Revelation 22:17)

> The Lord is not slack concerning his promise, as some men count slackness; but is longsuffering to us-ward, not

willing that any should perish, but that all should come to repentance. (2 Peter 3:9)

God certainly does not predestine any individual to be prevented entry into His kingdom. That entry is available to all. Thus none of us need despair. God's loving offer through His Holy Spirit and His church, symbolized here as the bride, is free to all.

As we said earlier in this book, we have "constructed" a mental dictionary which we term The *Standish Dictionary*. It occupies a very small segment of our feeble minds. It contains only very simple words. One of the words in the *Standish Dictionary* is **all**. In our dictionary the definition of **all** is very short—all. In our dictionary "all" does not mean "almost all," much less "few." "All" means "all!" Yet proponents of the doctrines of predestination dare to deny this fact, claiming that many humans are predestined to eternal damnation.

Nevertheless, Paul's prophecy above invites us to re-examine our connection with the God of heaven. He will not populate the New Earth, which He is preparing for His people, with those who so love sin that they wish to continue in it while claiming the right to dwell with God.

We trust Scripture; therefore, we must discard the false concept of God the Father being so centered upon wrath and punishment that He condemns to eternal torment those who choose to disregard His infinite offer when Scripture states otherwise in the plainest of terms:

> And to you who are troubled rest with us, when the Lord Jesus shall be revealed from heaven with his mighty angels, in flaming fire taking vengeance on them that know not God, and that obey not the gospel of our Lord Jesus Christ: who shall be punished with everlasting *destruction* from the presence of the Lord, and from the glory of his power. (2 Thessalonians 1:7–9)

> And they went up on the breadth of the earth, and compassed the camp of the saints about, and the beloved

city: and fire came down from God out of heaven, and *devoured* them. (Revelation 20:9)

The Bible here is precise. There is an eternal punishment for those who have not truly sought the Godhead's salvation. However, that punishment is eternal destruction. This same penalty will be meted out to Satan. Speaking of Satan in his heavenly role prior to his rebellion against God, Scripture refers to him as "the anointed cherub that covereth." (Ezekiel 28:14, 16) The prophet Ezekiel also saw his ultimate fate.

> Thou [Satan] hast defiled thy sanctuaries by the multitude of thine iniquities, by the iniquity of thy traffick; therefore will I bring forth a fire from the midst of thee, it shall devour thee, and I will bring thee to ashes upon the earth in the sight of all them that behold thee. All they that know thee among the people shall be astonished at thee: thou shalt be a terror, and never shalt thou be any more. (Ezekiel 28:18–19)

The word "vengeance" in the above passage from 2 Thessalonians must not be seen in human terms. The destruction of all unrepentant and unsanctified sinners is compatible with the very epitome of God's love. Heaven would be intolerable to those who prefer sin to righteousness.

The concept of eternal hell-fire was not a part of Christian thought in apostolic and early post-apostolic times. Christ, Himself, made the fate of those who rejected His salvation perfectly plain in a statement which is the most loved and most quoted in Scripture.

> For God so loved the world, that he gave his only begotten Son, that whosoever believeth in him should not *perish*, but have everlasting life. (John 3:16)

It puzzles many Christians that millions who sincerely quote this passage fail to see its significance in setting forth the fate of those who reject God's love.

The apostle Paul also taught the same fate of the lost in his emphasis on the resurrection of Christ as essential to our salvation.

> And if Christ be not raised, your faith is vain; ye are yet in your sins. Then they also which are fallen asleep in Christ are *perished*. (1 Corinthians 15:17–18)

Generally speaking, the Christian writers of the second century of the Christian era followed the biblical teaching that the fate of the unrepentant is eternal death. Thus the *Didache*, an early Christian book of faith, states that there are two ways—one leading to life, the other to death. (See *Didache* 1:1, 5:1)

In the second century, Clement, Bishop of Rome (Bishop 91–100) (not to be confused with Clement of Alexandria), wrote to the Corinthian church. In this letter, Clement quoted Acts 3:23, where Peter declared that

> transgressors will be cut off. (Acts 3:23, recorded in 1 Clement 14:3)

The writer of the so-called *Epistle of Barnabas,* written early in the second century, stated that the end of the world

> is near in which all things will perish with the Evil One. (*Barnabas* 21:3)

This writer also stated in this same "epistle" that the evildoer

> will perish together with his works. (*Barnabas* 21:1)

Another writer of the era, Ignatius of Antioch, wrote between 110 and 117,

> two things lie before us, life and death, and each person is about to go to his own place. (*Letter to Magnesians* 5:1)

Even though Justin Martyr attempted to integrate Greek philosophy with the Christian faith and thus had a confused theology, he did make statements indicative of his belief in the destruction of the soul. Three examples are quoted:

> Souls both die and are punished. (*First Apology*, chapter 5)

> The soul leaves the body, and the man exists no longer, even so whenever the soul must cease to exist, the spirit of life is removed from it. (*Ibid*, chapter 6)

> The fire of judgment would descend and utterly destroy all things. (*Ibid*, chapter 7)

Polycarp, (69–155) the well-known second century martyr,

> clearly taught that the wicked would be raised and judged. (Edward William Fudge, *The Fire that Consumes*, p. 320)

In the *Epistle of Diognetus* the author contrasted the first death with the second death of the wicked and stated that men will scorn the first death

> when they feel the real death, which is reserved for those who will be condemned to the eternal fire which will punish to the end those delivered over to it. (*Diognetus* 10:7)

The Mesopotamian, Tatian, who died in 180,

> denied that the soul was itself immortal. (Edward William Fudge, *op. cit.*, p. 327)

In his address to the Greeks, Tatian stated that

The soul itself is not immortal, O Greeks, but mortal.
(*Address to the Greeks*, chapter 13)

So through which avenue did the concept of a hateful God burning people eternally originate? Largely, it came from Greek philosophy which had absorbed it from Babylonian and other pagan religions. Speaking of the concept of the "immortality of the soul," Dr. Robert McAfee Brown (born 1920) is a Congregational pastor; a teacher at Amherst College, head of the department of religion, Macalister College, Minnesota; a professor of systematic theology, Union Theological Seminary, New York; and a member of the revision of the *Book of Common Worship* for the United Presbyterian Church. Brown traced this heathen concept from the Greeks:

> This is called "immortality of the soul." It comes from the Greeks, and when Greek thought and Hebrew-Christian thought came into contact in the early church, the Greek view often seemed to predominate. This view says, in effect, that there is a portion of me, my soul, that will continue to exist. During my lifetime here on earth this immortal soul is lodged in my mortal body. What happens at death is that my body dies and turns to dust, while my immortal soul is released and made free so that it can continue its immortal existence without being hamstrung by confinement in a body,
>
> Sounds pretty good, doesn't it? But wait a minute. This means that my body is a nuisance to my soul, something that confines it, limits it, hampers it, subjects it to temptation. As the Greeks themselves put it, "the body is the prison house of the soul." This means that life on earth in the body is a waste of time, an unpleasant interlude in the life of the soul, something to be over and done with as quickly as possible. The whole aim of life is to escape from life, get rid of the pesky body, in order to resume a free and unfettered existence in eternity. Human life on

earth has no final significance. (Dr. Robert Brown, *The Bible Speaks to You*, The Westminster Press, Philadelphia, 1955, pp. 221, 222)

Oscar Cullmann (born 1902), Protestant professor of the theological faculty of the University of Basel, Switzerland, and of the Sorbonne in Paris shared similar thoughts from his historical research:

> My critics belong to the most varied camps. The contrast, which out of concern for the truth I have found it necessary to draw between the courageous and joyful primitive Christian hope of the resurrection of the dead and the serene philosophic expectation of the survival of the immortal soul, has displeased not only many sincere Christians in all communions and of all theological outlooks, but also those whose convictions, while not outwardly alienated from Christianity, are more strongly molded by philosophical considerations. So far, no critic of either kind has attempted to refute me by exegesis, that being the basis of our study.
>
> This remarkable agreement seems to me to show how widespread is the mistake of attributing to primitive Christianity the Greek belief in the immortality of the soul. Further, people with such different attitudes as those I have mentioned are united in a common inability to *listen* with complete objectivity to what the texts teach us about the faith and hope of primitive Christianity, without mixing their own opinions and the views that are so dear to them with their interpretation of the texts. This inability to listen is equally surprising on the part of intelligent people committed to the principles of sound, scientific exegesis and on the part of believers who profess to rely on the revelation in Holy Scripture. (Dr. Oscar Cullman, *Immortality of the Soul or the Resurrection of the Dead?*, Macmillan, New York, 1958, pp. 5, 6)

The renowned Protestant Reformer, Martin Luther (1483–1546), himself a Roman Catholic monk, bore a strong testimony against the concept of the immortality of the soul, the foundation of the concept that unrepentant sinners will ever burn in hell:

> However I permit the Pope to establish articles of faith for himself and for his own faithful—such are: that the bread and wine are transubstantiated in the sacrament, that the Essence of God neither generates nor is generated, that the soul is the substantial form of the human body; that he [the pope] is emperor of the world and king of heaven, and earthly god; that the soul is immortal, and all these endless monstrous fictions [portenta] in the Roman rubbish heap of decretals—in order that such as his faith is, such may be his gospel, such also his faithful, and such his church, and that the lips may have similar lettuce and the lid may be worthy of the dish. (Martin Luther, *Assertion of all the Articles of M. Luther Condemned by the Newest Bull of Leo X*, Article 27 in his Works, Volume 7, Hermann Böhlhaus Nachfolger, Weimar, 1897, pp. 131, 132)

John Milton (1608–1674), English foreign minister, poet, and author of *Paradise Lost*, wrote extensively, exposing the pagans' irrational conclusion, accepted by Christians, that the soul survived after the death of the body. (See John Milton, *The Christian Doctrine* [George Bell and Sons, London, 1887], pp. 187–195)

The concept of the immortality of the soul, upon which the ever-burning sinner concept is predicated, denies the plain scriptural statement that the redeemed alone will receive immortality in their body which possesses a soul when Christ returns at the Second Advent.

> Now this I say, brethren, that flesh and blood cannot inherit the kingdom of God; neither doth corruption inherit incorruption. Behold, I shew you a mystery; We shall not all sleep, but we shall all be changed, in a moment, in the

twinkling of an eye, at the last trump: for the trumpet shall sound, and the dead shall be raised incorruptible, and we shall be changed. For this corruptible must put on incorruption, and this mortal must put on immortality. So when this corruptible shall have put on incorruption, and this mortal shall have put on immortality, then shall be brought to pass the saying that is written, Death is swallowed up in victory. (1 Corinthians 15:50–54)

Many miss the significance of Christ's promise to the dispirited apostles:

Let not your heart be troubled: ye believe in God, believe also in me. In my Father's house are many mansions: if it were not so, I would have told you. I go to prepare a place for you. And if I go and prepare a place for you, I will come again, and receive you unto myself; that where I am, there ye may be also. (John 14:1–3)

If the soul was immortal Christ most certainly would have pointed them to their respective deaths as the time they would be united with Him once more in His kingdom. But, on the contrary, He pointed to the moment when He would come again—the Second Coming—for that greatest of all reunions.

The prophet Nahum settled the issue when he reviewed the aim of the plan of salvation, as the eradication of affliction (sin) from the universe. Measure his words:

What do ye imagine against the Lord? he will make an utter end: affliction shall not rise up the second time. (Nahum 1:9)

If the soul was created immortal, then the curse of sin would have polluted the universe. The plan of salvation would be an utter failure. Christ's infinite sacrifice would have left the universe still unholy and vile.

John's words recorded in Revelation 21:4 that there would be no more pain, sorrow, nor tears, would be an utter falsehood, for such blights as the lost writhing in perpetual agony would greatly exceed those in our present-day sin-cursed earth.

> And God shall wipe away all tears from their eyes; and there shall be no more death, neither sorrow, nor crying, neither shall there be any more pain: for the former things are passed away. (Revelation 21:4)

Notice Nahum's penetrating question that we read above, which poses a rebuke: "What do ye imagine against the LORD?" Do we dare to speak of a heartless, all-powerful God who uses His omnipotence to torture un-repentant mankind and wicked angels for eternity? Do we dare to portray God as a being of infinite wisdom, while claiming He can never provide a solution to the sin problem which has blighted even the holiest place of the universe, Heaven itself? What a denigration it would be to our all-powerful, omniscient Father of love, if we, claiming to be His followers, would dare to answer either of the questions in the positive.

Nahum declares for all to read that God, praise His holy name, will "make an utter end." The day is coming when sin and sinners will be no more. Sin, we are assured, will not rise up a second time. God will not then make all His created beings into robots, unable to sin. The fact that sin did enter the universe is proof beyond all dispute that God created every being with a will and the power of choice and decision.

How would the authors feel when they receive lovely Fathers' Day cards from their children if those children were mere automatons who were programmed to send such words of love and appreciation? All would be emptiness.

Those who teach that all will be saved—universal salvation—do so in folly. God our Father would never force His love upon us or deprive His sentient beings of the power of choice and will. This doctrine was designed not in heaven but in the scheming mind of Satan.

So, too, is the doctrine of predestination. If God predestined us to either eternity in heaven or eternity in hell, He would be a God of partiality. What demonic spirit would bring humans into this world for a few years so that he could burn them for ever? It is incredible that such hateful attributes are ascribed to our God of love. We cannot be silent while such disgraceful words stand as slanders against our God. It is no wonder that these doctrines fail the scrutiny of Scripture.

In our book *The Mystery of Death* (see the list of Hartland Publications in the back of this book), we dispel the use of the terms eternal or everlasting as used in Scripture to bolster Satan's defamation of God that He tortures lost creatures for eternity.

CHAPTER 6

A Line of Truth

ECAUSE the Christian faith from the fourth century onward continued to adopt more concepts of paganism, cloaking them with a veneer of Christianity, our heavenly Father preserved the pure faith in small enclaves of Christian believers so that the flame of truth was never fully extinguished.

The most notable enclave devoted to the pure Christian faith was located in the rugged Alpine mountains and valleys of northwestern Italy, near the city of Turin. Here those true believers, who later became known as the Waldenses, nurtured the precious biblical truths.

> He [Peter Waldo] and his followers formed a center around which gathered the Arnoldisti and the Humiliati of Italy, the Petrobrusions and Albigensians of France, and perhaps the Apostolics of the Rhine Valley. . . . Some claimed Claude, Bishop of Turin (822–839) as their founder; others held that they were the successors of a small group of good men who had protested against the degradation of the Church in the days of Sylvester I [Pope, 314–335] and [Emperor] Constantine [280–337]. . . . It is certain, at all events, that the Waldensians of Piedmont were a fusion of various sects. (Ellen Scott Davison (died 1921), *Forerunners of St. Francis and Other Studies*, Edited by Gertrude R. B. Richards, Houghton Mifflin Company, Boston, 1927, pp. 237, 252, 253)

Ellen Davison was a specialist in historical research on the life of common people in the Middle Ages.

Another writer stated,

> Their [the Waldenses'] beginning we have fixed according to the common reckoning of ancient writers, A.D. 1170; but it appears that they existed long before. (Thieleman J. van Braght, *Martyrs Mirror*, p. 290)

Many of these Waldenses even kept the seventh-day Sabbath, which had virtually been extinguished in many parts of Europe after Constantine's "conversion," except in the Celtic churches of Great Britain and in Spain. By continuing to uphold the first day of the week, Sunday, as a special day, and encouraging Christians to hold it sacred alongside Saturday, Constantine put in place the ultimate replacement of the seventh day of the week for the first day of the week as the special day of worship for Christians. When error is mixed with truth it is inevitable that error will ultimately prevail. Thus was substituted Sunday, the pagan Roman day for veneration of their sun-god, in place of the biblical Seventh-day Sabbath.

Dr. Johann Joseph Ignaz von Döllinger, Th.D. (1799–1890) was a German Roman Catholic professor of church history and ecclesiastical law at the University of Munich who was excommunicated in 1871 when he rejected the Dogma of Papal Infallibility. He wrote,

> . . . not a few [Waldenses of the fifteenth century] celebrated the Sabbath with the Jews. (*Beitrage zur Sektengeschichte des Mittelalters* [Reports on the History of the Sects in the Middle Ages], Munich, 1890, second part, p. 661)

Other historians support the fact that many Waldensians kept the Sabbath.

> One of their [the Waldenses'] opinions, that the Law of Moses is to be kept according to the letter, and that the

keeping of the Sabbath . . . ought to take place. (Peter Allix, *The Ancient Churches of Piedmont*, Richard Chiswell, London, 1690, p. 154)

Observance of the Sabbath . . . is enjoined [by the Waldenses]. (Adam Blair, *History of the Waldenses*, Adam and Charles Black, Edinburgh, 1833, Vol. 1, p. 220)

God later turned to clerics of the Roman Catholic Church in order to bring His true teachings once more before professors of the Christian faith who were steeped in the ignorance of the Dark-Ages theology. Thus, as our Father chose prophets of old to return His chosen Jewish church from pagan practices during its more than 1,500 years of history, so did he use reformers from the fourteenth century forward, each adding more truth in order to "build the old waste places," and to "raise up the foundations of many generations" and to restore "the breach" and reconstruct the "paths to dwell in." (Isaiah 58:12)

The first of this line of reformers appeared in the Roman Catholic Church. John Wycliffe (1330–1384) arose in England and lived and died a Roman Catholic priest. He was consumed by God's Word and opened it to the populous of England through his translation, the first complete translation of the Bible into the English language. In 1995 the authors stood in John Wycliffe's church at Lutterworth and preached the pure Reformation faith. It was a privilege we will long remember. One of his Bibles was on display at the back of the church.

Wycliffe's work was carried on by another Roman Catholic priest, the Bohemian John Huss of Prague (1372–1415). He died a martyr. In 1997, we stood on the very spot where Huss was burned at the stake. That place of fearful sacrifice is presently located at the end of an ordinary suburban street in the city of Constance in southern Germany near the Swiss border. In 1994, we each ascended the high staircase in the Bethlehem Chapel in Prague, now a museum, where Huss had preached the reform faith to three thousand standing souls each week. Here we spoke, along with evangelist Raymond DeCarlo. Many of the visitors to the museum sat to listen to our presentations, which centered upon the completion of the Reformation prior to Christ's second coming. Our presentations were translated into the Czech language. A Czech mother and her adult daughter, visitors to the museum on that day, found the truths of Scripture and embraced the full faith of Jesus. They received more for their entrance fee than that for which they had bargained.

In the sixteenth century, the mighty Roman Catholic German monk, Martin (1483–1546), furthered the return to the apostolic faith. This was a century of great activity when four other mighty reformers rose to restore the truth—Huldrych (Ulrich) Zwingli (1484–1531), Guillaume Farel (1489–1565), John Knox (1505–1572), and John Calvin (1509–1564). Farel and Calvin were born in France, Zwingli in Switzerland, and Knox in Scotland. Each was educated in Roman Catholic institutions, and each served the Roman Catholic Church.

In the sixteenth century, it was the Geneva Bible, the Bishops' Bible, and the Tyndale New Testament, and in the seventeenth century it was the King James Version of the English Bible and other like translations in other languages which promoted and advanced the return to Bible truth, which had been so despoiled by the merging of pagan thought with the Christian faith during the Dark Ages.

In the eighteenth century, God turned to an Anglican minister, Englishman John Wesley (1703–1791) to forward the cause of truth which was in danger of being subverted once more as the zeal of the sixteenth-century Reformation markedly cooled.

By the nineteenth century God called an American Baptist lay pastor, William Miller (1782–1849) to rouse the people of God to sincere preparation for the second coming of the Lord.

A convert to Millers' rousing message was a young Methodist woman, Ellen Gould (Harmon) White (1827–1915). We have cited a passage of her writings in chapter two of this book. In this quintet, we will cite her further, for she developed into the greatest scriptural expositor of the nineteenth and twentieth centuries, and the most prolific author on any subject of that era. Born in Maine, in the United States, she visited numbers of European nations including Denmark, France, Germany, Italy, Norway, Sweden, Switzerland, and the United Kingdom. From 1891–1900 she lived in Australia and for a short period in New Zealand. Our maternal grandmother heard her speak in 1900.

Her perceptive writing, extending to almost twenty-five million words, covered virtually every aspect of Scripture and feature of Christian life.

CHAPTER 7

A Proper Evaluation of Our Father's Love

NO writer since the Apostle John laid down his pen for the last time around the year 100 AD, during his exile, has so perceptively evaluated the depth of the Father's love as set forth in God's Holy Word than this remarkable biblical expositor of the nineteenth and early twentieth centuries, Ellen Gould White.

This devout woman, so steeped in understanding of Scripture, despite her Methodist upbringing, soon discovered that the concept of eternal torment in hell was unbiblical and misrepresents God's character.

> Satan commenced his deception in Eden. He said to Eve, "Ye shall not surely die." This was Satan's first lesson upon the immortality of the soul, and he has carried on this deception from that time to the present, and will carry it on until the captivity of God's children shall be turned. (E. G. White, *Early Writings*, p. 218)

What had given Ellen White this understanding in contradiction to the belief of her mother church and the great theological weight of consensus of her day? It was, of course, the divine Word of God. Her biblical expositions were not the least influenced by current Christian thinking. She had determined to believe only the plain Word of God. In her tome on the history of Christianity and the culmination of end-time events, *The Great Controversy*, she explicitly set forth her position in 1911, just four years prior to her death at eighty-seven years of age, in respect to the revelation of Bible truth.

God will have a people upon the earth to maintain the Bible, and the Bible only, as the standard of all doctrines and the basis of all reforms. The opinions of learned men, the deductions of science, the creeds or decisions of ecclesiastical councils, as numerous and discordant as are the churches which they represent, the voice of the majority—not one nor all of these should be regarded as evidence for or against any point of religious faith. Before accepting any doctrine or precept, we should demand a plain "Thus saith the Lord" in its support. (E. G. White, *The Great Controversy*, p. 595)

What a difference it would make to understanding our Father if all Christian believers would follow this rule of exposition, rather than relying upon unscriptural traditions and propositions derived from the era of the Dark Ages when pagan thought merged with biblical enlightenment!

Listen to Mrs. White's clear thoughts upon the subject of the immortality of the soul, the pagan doctrine which forms the platform for the conjecture that God punishes the unrepentant sinner for ever in hell.

It was a marvel to me that Satan could succeed so well in making men believe that the words of God, "The soul that sinneth, it shall die," mean that the soul that sinneth it shall not die, but live eternally in misery. (E. G. White, *Early Writings*, p. 218)

In her above statement, Harmon-White relied upon a plain scriptural text:

The soul that sinneth, it shall die. The son shall not bear the iniquity of the father, neither shall the father bear the iniquity of the son: the righteousness of the righteous shall be upon him, and the wickedness of the wicked shall be upon him. (Ezekiel 18:20)

Who shall be punished with everlasting destruction from the presence of the Lord, and from the glory of his power. (2 Thessalonians 1:9)

And they went up on the breadth of the earth, and compassed the camp of the saints about, and the beloved city: and fire came down from God out of heaven, and devoured them. (Revelation 20:9)

She had discovered that life means life, whether it be a life of pain or happiness, and death means death, a state without pain, without joy, without hatred. It would be an amazing perversion of meaning if every occasion in which the Bible states that an individual had "died" it really means that he is actually *alive* in heaven, limbo, purgatory or hell.

In 1972, Russell was called urgently to the hospital in Malaysia where he was a physician. Upon arrival he saw a young woman of twenty-eight weeping uncontrollably beside an ambulance from another hospital.

That morning the young woman's thirty-four-year-old husband had left home on his bicycle as usual, to set up his primitive roadside coffee stall from which he made a minimal income to support his wife and their five children. About 10 a.m. he had collapsed and was rushed to another hospital. A serious brain hemorrhage was diagnosed, and the clinical signs were such that the physician in charge of the case concluded that there was no hope for recovery. Because the hospital where the patient was taken was overcrowded, it was reluctantly decided to send the patient home to die. The physician predicted the sufferer would die before the next dawn.

As the ambulance sped toward the man's home, the distraught wife pleaded with the driver to take him to the "Mission Hospital" (Penang Adventist Hospital) in the desperate hope that the life of her husband could be saved. Russell was a young thirty-eight-year-old specialist in internal medicine at the time and at the height of his medical skills. He thoroughly examined the man and concluded the same doleful prognosis as the physician in the government hospital. Death, he felt, was only a few hours away. It was agreed to retain this poor man in the hospital until it was necessary to write his death certificate.

But there is a great God in heaven! With the chaplain, Pastor John Lai, Russell prayed for the life of that man, and he was miraculously healed, regaining consciousness quite suddenly one week later. Mr. Gan lived to become a grandfather. What experiences did this man have during his one week of deep coma? Precisely none! Indeed, it was only with the greatest difficulty that it was possible to convince Mr. Gan that a week had elapsed since his collapse. He had absolutely no sense of the passage of time and was dogmatic that it was still the day of the onset of his illness. This is the usual reaction of patients emerging from comas. We see a similar situation with the majority of persons awaking from a general anesthetic of many hours duration.

Where, we well may ask, is the "soul" in these countless cases? We have highlighted Mr. Gan's experience because he accepted Christ after his illness, having previously been a devout Buddhist. He became a church deacon. However, his is just a typical experience. If the soul (consciousness) does not depend upon a functioning brain for its existence, where is it in the comatose patient? It certainly challenges logic to suggest that while there is no consciousness in a dysfunctional brain, yet when a brain ceases to function altogether, then consciousness returns. Or should we simply be content with Scripture, which repeatedly states that death is a sleep? Presumably, when Adam arises on the resurrection morning, he will not sense the passage of time, and he will be initially surprised that Christ returned "so promptly."

Mrs. White perceptively pointed out that:

> As the error [of the immortality of the soul] was received by the people, and they were led to believe that man was immortal, Satan led them on to believe that the sinner would live in eternal misery. Then the way was prepared for Satan to work through his representatives and hold up God before the people as a revengeful tyrant—one who plunges all those into hell who do not please Him, and causes them ever to feel His wrath; and while they suffer unutterable anguish, and writhe in the eternal flames, He is represented as looking down upon them with satisfac-

tion. Satan knew that if this error should be received, God would be hated by many, instead of being loved and adored; and that many would be led to believe that the threatenings of God's Word would not be literally fulfilled, for it would be against His character of benevolence and love to plunge into eternal torments the beings whom He had created. (E. G. White, *Early Writings*, pp. 218–219)

The same scriptural expositor set forth several consequences of denying that the sinner is destroyed in the Day of Judgment, but rather lives on eternally in hell. Naturally, many thinking people find it impossible to reconcile the God of love with such a vile act as to punish punitively the wicked forever without hope of relief from this suffering. We cite other doctrinal errors Mrs. White sets out as having been crafted in the light of the contrast of the God of love and His supposed eternal torment of the wicked.

Another extreme which Satan has led the people to adopt is entirely to overlook the justice of God, and the threatenings in His Word, and to represent Him as being all mercy, so that not one will perish, but that all, both saint and sinner, will at last be saved in His kingdom.

In consequence of the popular errors of the immortality of the soul and endless misery, Satan takes advantage of another class and leads them to regard the Bible as an uninspired book. They think it teaches many good things; but they cannot rely upon it and love it, because they have been taught that it declares the doctrine of eternal misery.

Another class Satan leads on still further, even to deny the existence of God. They can see no consistency in the character of the God of the Bible, if He will inflict horrible tortures upon a portion of the human family to all eternity. Therefore they deny the Bible and its Author and regard death as an eternal sleep.

There is still another class who are fearful and timid. These Satan tempts to commit sin, and after they have sinned, he holds up before them that the wages of sin is not death but life in horrible torments, to be endured throughout the endless ages of eternity. By thus magnifying before their feeble minds the horrors of an endless hell, he takes possession of their minds, and they lose their reason. Then Satan and his angels exult, and the infidel and atheist join in casting reproach upon Christianity. They claim that these evils are the natural results of believing in the Bible and its Author, whereas they are the results of the reception of popular heresy. (*Ibid*, pp. 219–220.)

Addressing Christian pastors on a different subject, Mrs. White provided a word of proper counsel that equally applies regarding our topic of discussion:

Men think they are representing the justice of God, but they do not represent His tenderness and the great love wherewith He has loved us. (E. G. White, *Testimonies to Ministers*, p. 363)

The authors are both ordained pastors. What a warning this is to us! Of course, God is a God of perfect justice; to this Scripture fully testifies. But without presuming on His love to save us while we defy His law, we must ever trust His tender love to provide us with power to serve Him in obedience to His law and to fill our hearts with the joy of His salvation.

Mrs. White fully weighed Christ's words concerning our Father. Christ had declared to His disciples,

Ye neither know me, nor my Father: if ye had known me, ye should have known my Father also. (John 8:19)

Christ had answered the Apostle Philip's request to know more about the Father:

Philip saith unto him, Lord, shew us the Father, and it sufficeth us. Jesus saith unto him, Have I been so long time with you, and yet hast thou not known me, Philip? he that hath seen me hath seen the Father; and how sayest thou then, Shew us the Father? Believest thou not that I am in the Father, and the Father in me? the words that I speak unto you I speak not of myself: but the Father that dwelleth in me, he doeth the works. Believe me that I am in the Father, and the Father in me: or else believe me for the very works' sake. (John 14:8–11)

None can doubt the love of Christ. Yet many wrongly see the Father as a stern, unyielding, vengeful being. This Mrs. White, commenting on the above verses, fully discerned:

"If ye had known Me," Christ said, "ye should have known My Father also: and from henceforth ye know Him, and have seen Him." But not yet did the disciples understand. "Lord, show us the Father," exclaimed Philip, "and it sufficeth us."

Amazed at his dullness of comprehension, Christ asked with pained surprise, "Have I been so long time with you, and yet hast thou not known Me, Philip?" Is it possible that you do not see the Father in the works He does through Me? Do you not believe that I came to testify of the Father? "How sayest thou then, Show us the Father?" "He that hath seen Me hath seen the Father." Christ had not ceased to be God when He became man. Though He had humbled Himself to humanity, the Godhead was still His own. Christ alone could represent the Father to humanity, and this representation the disciples had been privileged to behold for over three years.

"Believe Me that I am in the Father, and the Father in Me: or else believe Me for the very works' sake." Their faith might safely rest on the evidence given in Christ's works, works that no man, of himself, ever had done, or ever could do. Christ's work testified to His divinity. Through Him the Father had been revealed. (E. G. White, *The Desire of Ages*, pp. 663–664)

Representing the Father's character as an example to each of His followers, Mrs. White stated,

All the varied capabilities that men possess—of mind and soul and body—are given them by God, to be so employed as to reach the highest possible degree of excellence. But this cannot be a selfish and exclusive culture; for the character of God, whose likeness we are to receive, is benevolence and love. Every faculty, every attribute, with which the Creator has endowed us is to be employed for His glory and for the uplifting of our fellow men. And in this employment is found its purest, noblest, and happiest exercise. (E. G. White, *Patriarchs and Prophets*, p. 595)

Once more Mrs. White has carefully enunciated the biblical principle of our heavenly Example. How different is this understanding of God from that of many twenty-first century thinkers. "Benevolence and love" fully represent our God's character, and such qualities He is ever willing to bestow upon His followers.

When we see the wonderful character of God it encourages us to seek His freely offered grace in order to reflect that character as loving, compassionate children of His.

Be ye therefore perfect, even as your Father which is in heaven is perfect. (Matthew 5:48)

Notice Mrs. White's evaluation of this principle:

God will accept only those who are determined to aim high. He places every human agent under obligation to do his best. Moral perfection is required of all. Never should we lower the standard of righteousness in order to accommodate inherited or cultivated tendencies to wrong-doing. We need to understand that imperfection of character is sin. All righteous attributes of character dwell in God as a perfect, harmonious whole, and every one who receives Christ as a personal Saviour is privileged to possess these attributes.

And those who would be workers together with God must strive for perfection of every organ of the body and quality of the mind. True education is the preparation of the physical, mental, and moral powers for the performance of every duty; it is the training of body, mind, and soul for divine service. This is the education that will endure unto eternal life. (E. G. White, *Christ's Object Lessons*, p. 330)

The inspired words of the mighty prophet, Moses recommend themselves to us today:

And let the beauty of the LORD our God be upon us: and establish thou the work of our hands upon us; yea, the work of our hands establish thou it. (Psalm 90:17)

CHAPTER 8

Depictions of God's Eternal Torment

MRS. White, later in life, reflected graphically upon her childhood education by Methodist ministers who set forth the terrors of eternal hell.

In my mind the justice of God eclipsed His mercy and love. The mental anguish I passed through at this time was very great. I had been taught to believe in an eternally burning hell; and as I thought of the wretched state of the sinner without God, without hope, I was in deep despair. I feared that I should be lost, and that I should live throughout eternity suffering a living death. The horrifying thought was ever before me, that my sins were too great to be forgiven, and that I should be forever lost.

The frightful descriptions that I had heard of souls in perdition sank deep into my mind. Ministers in the pulpit drew vivid pictures of the condition of the lost. They taught that God proposed to save none but the sanctified; that the eye of God was upon us always; that God Himself was keeping the books with the exactness of infinite wisdom; and that every sin we committed was faithfully registered against us, and would meet its just punishment.

Satan was represented as eager to seize upon his prey, and bear us to the lowest depths of anguish, there to exult over our sufferings in the horrors of an eternally burning hell, where, after the tortures of thousands upon thousands of years, the fiery billows would roll to the surface the writhing victims, who would shriek, "How long, O Lord, how long?" Then the answer would thunder down the abyss, "Through all eternity!" Again the molten waves would engulf the lost, carrying them down into the depths of an ever restless sea of fire.

While listening to these terrible descriptions, my imagination would be so wrought upon that the perspiration would start, and it was difficult to suppress a cry of anguish, for I seemed already to feel the pains of perdition. Then the minister would dwell upon the uncertainty of life: one moment we might be here, and the next in hell; or one moment on earth, and the next in heaven. Would we choose the lake of fire and the company of demons, or the bliss of heaven with angels for our companions? Would we hear the voice of wailing and the cursing of lost souls through all eternity, or sing the songs of Jesus before the throne?

Our heavenly Father was presented before my mind as a tyrant, who delighted in the agonies of the condemned; not as the tender, pitying Friend of sinners, who loves His creatures with a love past all understanding, and desires them to be saved in His kingdom.

When the thought took possession of my mind that God delighted in the torture of His creatures, who were formed in His image, a wall of darkness seemed to separate me from Him. When I reflected that the Creator of the universe would plunge the wicked into hell, there to burn through the ceaseless rounds of eternity, my heart sank with fear, and I despaired that so cruel and tyrannical a being would ever condescend to save me from the doom of sin.

I thought that the fate of the condemned sinner would be mine—to endure the flames of hell forever, even as long as God Himself existed. Almost total darkness settled upon me, and there seemed no way out of the shadows. Could the truth have been presented to me as I now understand it, much perplexity and sorrow would have been spared me. If the love of God had been dwelt upon more, and His stern justice less, the beauty and glory of His character would have inspired me with a deep and earnest love for my Creator. (E. G. White, *Life Sketches*, pp. 29–31)

Mrs. White's childhood terrors have not been the lot only of children. Countless millions of adults over past centuries have held such torments of mind. Only Christ's infinite love draws us to Him in peace. The fear of eternal torture does not.

> For the love of Christ constraineth us; because we thus judge, that if one died for all, then were all dead. (2 Corinthians 5:14)

It was not only Protestantism which sought to terrify its communicants into a life of spiritual rectitude, but also Roman Catholicism.

Some Christians present hell as the domain of devils and even accord them the right to judge the sinners. One such view declared that

> The devils carry away the soul which has just come into hell. They bear it through the flames. Now they have set it down in front of the great chained monster, to be judged by him, who has no mercy. Oh, that horrible face of the devil! Oh, the fright, the shivering, the freezing, the deadly horror of that soul at the first sight of the great devil. Now the devil opens his mouth. He gives out the tremendous sentence on the soul. All hear the sentence, and hell rings with shouts of spiteful joy and mockeries at the unfortunate soul. (J. Furniss, *Tracts for Spiritual Reading*, New York, P. J. Kennedy, Excelsior Catholic Publishing House, 1882, p. 12)

Attempts have been made to terrify children into a life of righteousness:

The devil gave Job one stroke, only one stroke. That one stroke was so terrible that it covered all his body with sores and ulcers. That one stroke made Job look so frightful, that his friends did not know him again. That one stroke was so terrible, that for seven days and seven nights his friends did not speak a word, but sat crying, and wondering, and thinking what a terrible stroke the devil can give. (*Ibid*, p. 13)

Little child, if you go to hell there will be a devil at your side to strike you. He will go on striking you every minute for ever and ever, without ever stopping. The first stroke will make your body as bad as the body of Job, covered from head to foot with sores and ulcers. The second stroke will make your body twice as bad as the body of Job. The third stroke will make your body three times as bad as the body of Job. The fourth stroke will make your body four times as bad as the body of Job. How then will your body be after the devil has been striking it every moment for a hundred million years without stopping?

But there was one good thing for Job. When the devil had struck Job, his friends came to visit and comfort him, and when they saw him they cried. But when the devil is striking you in hell, there will be no one to come and visit and comfort you, and cry with you. Neither father, nor mother, nor brother, nor sister, nor friend will ever come to cry with you. [Lamentations 1:2] "Weeping she hath wept in the night, and the tears on her cheeks, because there is none to comfort her amongst all them that were dear to her." Little child, it is a bad bargain to make with the devil, to commit a mortal sin, and then to be beaten for ever for it. (*Ibid*, p. 14)

Another effort to subject young people to the will of God is cited:

Look into this room. What a dreadful place it is! The roof is red hot; the walls are red hot; the floor is like a thick sheet of red hot iron. See, on the middle of that red hot floor stands a girl. She looks about sixteen years old. Her feet are bare, she has neither shoes nor stockings on her feet; her bare feet stand on the red hot burning floor. The door of this room has never been opened before since she first set her foot on the red hot floor. Now she sees that the door is opening. She speaks! She says; "I have been standing with my bare feet on this red hot floor for years. Day and night my only standing place has been this red hot floor. Sleep never came on me for a moment, that I might forget this horrible burning floor. Look," she says, "at my burnt and bleeding feet. Let me go off this burning floor for one moment, only for one single, short moment. Oh, that in the endless eternity of years, I might forget the pain only for one single moment." The devil answers her question: "Do you ask," he says, "for a moment, for one moment to forget your pain? No, not for one single moment during the never-ending eternity of years shall you ever leave this red hot floor!" "Is it so?" the girl says with a sigh, that seems to break her heart; "then, at least, let somebody go to my little brothers and sisters, who are alive, and tell them not to do the bad things which I did, so they will never have to come and stand on the red hot floor." The devil answers her again: "Your little brothers and sisters have the priests to tell them these things. If they will not listen to the priests, neither would they listen even if somebody should go to them from the dead."

Oh, that you could hear the horrible, the fearful scream of that girl when she saw the door shutting, never to be opened any more. The history of this girl is short. Her feet first led her into sin, so it is her feet which, most of all, are tormented. While yet a very little child, she began to go into bad company. The more she grew up, the more she went into bad company against the bidding of her parents. She used to walk about the streets at night, and do very wicked things. She died early. Her death was brought on by the bad life she led. (*Ibid*, p. 19)

Each of the above descriptions was published in 1882 in New York by the Excelsior Catholic Publishing House.

Non-Christians have similar views.

Dr. Peter de Rosa, a "graduate of the Gregorian University, Rome, was Professor of Metaphysics and Ethics at Westminster [Roman Catholic] Seminary, [England] for six years and Dean of Theology at Corpus Christi [Roman Catholic College, London] for six years." (Peter de Rosa, *Vicars of Christ*, Corgi Books, 1989, page ii of frontispiece), stated:

> According to the age-long tradition, formulated by [St] Augustine [(354–430)] and sanctioned by Pope St. Gregory [I] and all his successors, baptism was a prerequisite of salvation. Day-old babies born of Christian parents went to hell if they died unbaptized. So did catechumens if they died unexpectedly. Of course, the entire pagan world was doomed to damnation. According to Augustine, even the Good Thief was only saved because in some unspecified way he was baptized.
>
> There is no better proof of the church's fallibility than this. It is not as if pontiffs and fathers said they did not know how babies could be saved; they said categorically it was impossible. They did not plead ignorance of the fate of the mass of mankind who had never heard of Christ; they affirmed without qualification that they all went to hell. There was no salvation outside the church; and by the church they meant the Catholic church wherein entry was gained *only* by baptism of water. These views were repeated century after century without one dissenting voice. It was Catholic teaching, taught always, everywhere, by everyone. We noticed that when St. Francis Xavier [1506–1552] went to the Indies he was certain that unbaptized pagans, *however virtuous*, could not get to heaven.

The hard-heartedness of Christians of earlier generations astonished everyone today, but whatever the rea-
sons, it is a fact. Any Catholic who doubted it would have
been burned by the Inquisition. According to Dr. William
Lecky, this teaching surpassed in atrocity any tenet ad-
opted by pagans. It merited Tacitus' tag of a 'pernicious
superstition.' Lecky writes:

"That a little child who lives but a few minutes after
birth and dies before it has been sprinkled with the sacred
water is in such a sense responsible for its ancestor having
six thousand years before eaten a forbidden fruit, that it
may with perfect justice be resuscitated and cast into an
abyss of eternal fire in expiation of this ancestral crime,
that an all-righteous and merciful Creator, in the full exercise of these attributes, deliberately calls into existence
sentient beings whom He had from eternity irrevocably
destined to endure unspeakable, unmitigated torture, are
propositions which are at once so extravagantly absurd
and so ineffably atrocious that their adoption might well
lead men to doubt the universality of moral perception.
Such teaching is, in fact, simply demonism, and demonism
in its most extreme form."

Extreme demonism or not, it was Catholic orthodoxy
until almost modern times. God's image never emerged
more tarnished from a witch's manual. The most monstrous of human cruelties perpetrated by Attila the Hun
or Adolf Hitler pale in comparison with the cruelties attributed by gentle Christian theologians and contemplative
monks to God the Father of Our Lord Jesus Christ. In fact
not even the devil has been painted in such lurid colors.

The real mystery is why Christians have held these
views for so long. There is only one answer: authority. The
authority of the Bible, in the first instance, but the Bible
as interpreted by the teachers of the church (the magiste-
rium). Paul's mystical words, 'In Adam all have sinned,'

were boneheadedly taken to imply that even newborn babies were responsible for original sin and doomed to hell if they died unbaptized.

Christians who would never have forgiven themselves if they had injured a child gratuitously were content to think that God would punish him with unspeakable and eternal torments for something which was not in his power to avoid. We would think that no Christian parent in his or her heart could possibly have believed this monstrous lie; but many assented to it. It is perhaps the best example in history of Catholic authority, without reason or humanity on its side, demanding obedience to a morally, absurd, non-biblical doctrine. As Lecky also remarked:

"Christians esteem it a matter of duty and a commend-able exercise of humility, to stifle the moral feelings of their nature, and they at last succeed in persuading them-selves that their Divinity would be extremely offended if they hesitated to ascribe to Him the attributes of a fiend. . . . Their doctrine is accepted as a kind of moral miracle, and, as is customary with a certain school of theologians, when they enunciate a proposition that is palpably self-contradictory, they call it a mystery and an occasion of faith." (*Ibid*, pp. 460, 461)

Here we see that a canonized Pontiff, one held in highest esteem in the Roman Catholic Church, presented our Father as a merciless deity who was prepared to torture little babies for ever in hell, simply because their parents had neglected to christen them.

Other popes made unfortunate pronouncements. Greg-ory the Great said that unbaptized babies go straight to hell and suffer there for all eternity. Some pontiffs went further. [St] Innocent I (401–17) wrote to the Council of Milevis and [St] Gelasius I (492–6) wrote to the Bishop of Picenum that babies were obliged to receive communion.

If they died baptized but uncommunicated, they would go straight to hell. (*Ibid*, de Rosa, p. 289)

Some Protestant denominations, believing the twin doctrines of eternal punishment in hell and that God predestinates some humans to hell and others to heaven, also dare to defame our God of love as a being who permits humans to be born for whom no hope of eternal life is offered. These unfortunate ones, they say, are divinely predestined to burn in excruciating agony not for a second, a minute, a day, a week, a month, a year, a decade, a century, a millennium, a million years, a billion years, but for eternity. How can clerics present such extreme distortions of the character of our loving Father? God is not partial, selecting some arbitrarily for heaven and others for hell. He offers salvation to all:

The Lord is . . . not willing that any should perish, but that all should come to repentance. (2 Peter 3:9)

Let us therefore come boldly unto the throne of grace, that we may obtain mercy, and find grace to help in time of need. (Hebrews 4:16)

And the Spirit and the bride say, Come. And let him that heareth say, Come. And let him that is athirst come. And whosoever will, let him take the water of life freely. (Revelation 22:17)

With such portrayals of our Father as we have reviewed in this chapter, is it any marvel that millions of thinking individuals have discarded Christianity, that many have never experienced the love of God, and that infidels scorn such a God? This representation of God's insatiable wrath, of course, bears no resemblance to our heavenly Father; rather it reveals the character of Satan who, if in possession of this power, would treat humans in this manner.

Accepting this doctrine, is it any wonder that God's tender, loving words to us have been lost on the minds of many?

But God commendeth his love toward us, in that, while we were yet sinners, Christ died for us. . . . For if, when we were enemies, we were reconciled to God by the death of his Son, much more, being reconciled, we shall be saved by his life. (Romans 5:8, 10)

Praise God, He, unlike Satan, is love.

CHAPTER 9

God Defamed by Indulgences

THE unscriptural notion of the immortality of the soul was compli-
cated by the doctrine not only of an ever-burning hell, but also that
of purgatory. Neither place is described in Scripture, for neither
exists. Revelation reveals the final fate of the unrepentant wicked. Chapter
twenty of the last book of the Holy Bible speaks of the resurrection of
the wicked dead, describing it as the second resurrection.

But let us examine this within the context of the resurrection of the
saints of all the ages. The redeemed are raised at the Second Coming in
the First Resurrection.

> For the Lord himself shall descend from heaven with a
> shout, with the voice of the archangel, and with the trump
> of God: and the dead in Christ shall rise first. (1 Thes-
> salonians 4:16)

The Bible specifically calls this the "First Resurrection":

> But the rest of the dead lived not again until the thou-
> sand years were finished. This is the first resurrection.
> (Revelation 20:5)

Speaking of the destruction at the Second Coming of the wicked all
of whom had followed the "man of sin," a synonym for the antichrist,
Scripture clearly attests to their fate:

> And then shall that Wicked be revealed, whom the
> Lord shall consume with the spirit of his mouth, and
> shall destroy with the brightness of his coming: even
> him, whose coming is after the working of Satan with all
> power and signs and lying wonders, and with all deceiv-
> ableness of unrighteousness in them that perish; because
> they received not the love of the truth, that they might be
> saved. (2 Thessalonians 2:8–10)

Nevertheless the Word of God in clear terms reveals that this is not
the final fate of the wicked. After describing the reward of the righteous,
the Bible compares the awful "reward" of the wicked:

> And I saw thrones, and they sat upon them, and judg-
> ment was given unto them: and I saw the souls of them
> that were beheaded for the witness of Jesus, and for the
> word of God, and which had not worshipped the beast,
> neither his image, neither had received his mark upon
> their foreheads, or in their hands; and they lived and
> reigned with Christ a thousand years. But the rest of
> the dead lived not again until the thousand years were
> finished. This is the first resurrection. . . . And death
> and hell were cast into the lake of fire. This is the sec-
> ond death. And whosoever was not found written in the
> book of life was cast into the lake of fire. (Revelation
> 20:4–15)

It is our merciful heavenly Father who annihilates the final unrepentant, who would otherwise continue to sow discord, unhappiness,
and revolt within the universe. They would never live happily in a pure
world, just as their leader brought misery to the entire heavenly host by
his initial rebellion. When the wicked are raised in the second resurrection, they seek to destroy God's redeemed saints who have descended in
the city—the New Jerusalem—to the earth. At this moment the wicked
are destroyed eternally by heavenly fire.

And they went up on the breadth of the earth, and compassed the camp of the saints about, and the beloved city: and fire came down from God out of heaven, and devoured them. And the devil that deceived them was cast into the lake of fire and brimstone, where the beast and the false prophet are, and shall be tormented day and night for ever and ever. (Revelation 20:9–10)

We will later revisit this term "ever and ever," for many seize upon this term to support the concept of unending punishment in hell, overlooking that the ninth verse plainly declares that Satan and his followers are "devoured" by God's fire.

Numerous Christians have sacrificed huge sums of money to extricate their loved ones from the supposed punishment meted out in purgatory. This "place" is not referred to in Holy Writ. This place is non-existent, so no one has ever entered or left it.

The Roman Catholic Council of Trent (1545–1563), not withstanding the total absence of the notion of purgatory in Scripture, dared to assert that

Whereas the Catholic Church, instructed by the Holy Ghost, has, from the Sacred Writings and the ancient tradition of the Fathers, taught in sacred councils, and very recently in this ecumenical synod that there is a Purgatory, and that the souls there detained are helped by the suffrages of the faithful, but principally by the acceptable sacrifice of the altar; the holy synod enjoins on bishops that they diligently endeavor that the sound doctrine concerning Purgatory, transmitted by the holy Fathers and sacred councils, be believed, maintained, taught and everywhere proclaimed by the faithful of Christ. (Council of Trent, Session XXV (Dec. 3 and 4, 1563), Decree Concerning Purgatory, in *Dogmatic Canons and Decrees,* p. 165. Copyright 1912 by the Devin-Adair Company, New York)

The Roman Catholic Church appears to lack "knowledge" of the period of time spent in purgatory. American Jesuit writer, Dr. Joseph Husslein (1873–1952), a contributor to the *Catholic Encyclopedia*, wrote,

> While Purgatory itself is limited by the last judgment, we cannot speak with equal certainty of the length of time during which individual souls may have to undergo their purification, that they be rendered fit to enter into the sight of the All-Holy God. The duration of Purgatory may extend for some over many years. Of this we are practically certain, since it is the custom of the Church herself to offer up anniversary Masses for individual souls during hundreds of years. (Joseph Husslein, *The Souls in Purgatory,* p. 21. Copyright 1924 by The America Press, New York)

This accounts for the fact that in the year 2000, when the Olympic Games were hosted by Sydney, Australia, and the Olympic torch relay reached Melbourne, a special prayer for the soul of a 1956 Italian Olympic road cyclist was offered at a Melbourne Roman Catholic Church. This young man had been killed in a road accident just prior to the opening of the 1956 Olympic Games. So it was imagined that this poor young man was still in the miseries of purgatory in 2000, forty-four years later.

As with other non-scriptural concepts that entered Christian theology in the Dark Ages, the origin of purgatory is pagan.

> An analogy to purgatory can be traced in most [pagan] religions. Zoroaster conducts souls through 12 stages before they are sufficiently purified to enter heaven; on the stories conceived of a middle place of enlightenment which they called *empurosis*. (*Encyclopaedia Britannica*, 1963 Edition, Vol. 18, p. 775B)

The same encyclopedia defined purgatory as

A state of suffering after death in which the souls of those who die in venial sin, and of those who still owe some debt of temporal punishment for mortal sin, are rendered fit to enter heaven. It is believed that such souls continue to be members of the church of Christ; that they are helped by the suffrages of the living—that is, by prayers, alms and other good works, and more especially by the sacrifice of the mass; and that, although delayed until "the last farthing is paid," their salvation is assured. Catholics support this doctrine chiefly by reference to the Jewish belief in the efficacy of prayer for the dead (2 Macc., xii, 42 *seq), the tradition of the early Christians and the authority of the church.

The state of purgatory is usually thought of as having some position in space, and as being distinct from heaven and hell; but any theory as to its exact latitude and longitude, such as underlies Dante Alighieri's description, must be regarded as imaginative.

Most theologians since [St] Thomas Aquinas [(1225–1274)] and St. Bonaventura [(1221–1274)] have taught that the souls in purgatory are tormented by material fire. . . . (Ibid.)

In the early sixteenth century Johann Tetzel, (1465–1519), a German Dominican monk, awarded indulgences to all who paid for them. He made incredible claims. In the mining region of St. Annaberg, Tetzel declared that if the populace

contributed readily and bought grace and indulgence, all the hills of St. Annaberg would become pure massive silver. (Translation quoted in Oliver J. Thatcher and Edgar Holmes McNeal, eds., *A Source Book for Mediaeval History,* pp. 338–340. Copyright 1905, Charles Scribner's Sons; renewal copyright 1933, Oliver J. Thatcher)

He also claimed that

> as soon as the coin clinked in the chest, the soul for
> whom the money was paid would go straight to heaven.
> (Ibid.)

Huge amounts of money gathered by Tetzel helped to construct St. Peter's Basilica in Rome. (See instruction from the Archbishop of Mainz, Germany, to Tetzel, *Reprints From the Original Sources of European History,* Vol. 2, No. 6, Philadelphia: University of Pennsylvania Press, p. 5)

Surely the concept of purgatory and its association with the payment of money for the release of souls from that fictitious place shames the name of our pure and holy Father. God surely freely extends His grace to all who truly repent.

> If we confess our sins, he is faithful and just to forgive
> us our sins, and to cleanse us from all unrighteousness.
> (1 John 1:9)

Yet even when Pope John Paul II revisited the touchy arena of indulgences, the matter which had caused the greatest schism in the Roman Catholic Church, he came out virtually unscathed. The Lutheran Church had made its peace with the Vatican, and it seemed that no man of the caliber of its founder arose almost five centuries later to nail his ninety-five theses on the church door. Protestantism's protest was not even a whimper as, year by year, the ecumenical movement, having dulled Protestant sensibilities, saw the popularity of John Paul soar.

John Paul's papal bull, *Incarnationis Mysterium* (The Mystery of the Incarnation), was interpreted to state that,

> During the millennium celebration, penitents who do
> a charitable deed or give up cigarettes or alcohol for a
> day can earn an "indulgence" that will eliminate time in
> purgatory. (*International Herald Tribune*—an overseas

newspaper compiled by the *Washington Post* and *New York Times*—November 29, 1998)

As the newspaper reported,

> The Medieval church sold indulgences, a practice which drove Martin to rebel and begin the Reformation. They remain a source of intense debate between Protestants and Catholics, and since Vatican II the church has played down their importance. (Ibid.)

John Paul ensured that no longer would indulgences be played down. Indeed, in this bold act, rather than increasing the rift between Rome and Protestantism he was

> broadening the ways believers can earn an indulgence beyond traditional Catholic rituals . . . trying to imbue indulgences with some of the ecumenical spirit he wants to lend the celebrations. (Ibid.)

The *International Herald Tribune* need not have concerned itself with "intense debate between Protestant and Catholics." In contrast to the sixteenth century, the papal bull, was taken on board by most Protestants as if it did not matter. Campbell Reid, the editor of the nationwide Rupert Murdoch-owned newspaper, *The Australian*, in his editorial of December 2, 1998, commented,

> Of course, whatever criticism the granting of indulgences attracts, the encouragement to live a better life must find widespread commendation.

There was no sense that men's souls were at stake, that devout Catholics, unmindful of Scripture, would believe that such indulgences absolved their sins and would be drawn further to believe in the unbiblical concept of purgatory.

John Paul had tested the winds and found them gently blowing toward Rome. That which produced a seismic shock wave of gigantic proportions in 1517 did not elicit more than the slightest ripple in 1998, 481 years later.

On May 13, 1999, the electronic London *Telegraph* reported that,

> The pope was recognized as the overall authority in the Christian world by an Anglican and Roman Catholic Commission yesterday which described him as a "gift to be received by all the churches." . . . The commission concluded that the Bishop of Rome had a "specific ministry concerning the discernment of truth." . . . The Rt. Rev. Cormac Murphy-O'Connor, Bishop of Arundel and Brighton [now Cardinal Archbishop of Westminster] and the . . . co-chairman added: "The primacy of the Pope is a gift to be shared."

By contrast, God extends His grace of forgiveness without price. Indulgences misrepresent God's love and present Him as a scheming deity, desiring to strip us of our livelihood. It is a gross and evil caricature of our Father's generous love, freely bestowed. Listen to His Word:

> For all have sinned, and come short of the glory of God; being justified freely by his grace through the redemption that is in Christ Jesus: whom God hath set forth to be a propitiation through faith in his blood, to declare his righteousness for the remission of sins that are past, through the forbearance of God. (Romans 3:23–25)

While the concept of indulgences has been a tremendous money-maker for Roman Catholic clerics for centuries, it denies the very character of our Father of love. The Bible does not support the concept of purgatory after death to purify our character to fit us for heaven. Each of us must respond to Christ's loving invitation during our life on earth prior to death. Our characters are sealed for eternity either for eternal life or for eternal destruction at death. We make the decision whether to follow our loving Saviour to eternal life or to follow Satan to eternal destruction.

CHAPTER 10

The Quandary of Ever and Ever

S CRIPTURE speaks of everlasting and eternal fire. Christ, Himself, spoke in such terms:

> Wherefore if thy hand or thy foot offend thee, cut them off, and cast them from thee: it is better for thee to enter into life halt or maimed, rather than having two hands or two feet to be cast into everlasting fire. And if thine eye offend thee, pluck it out, and cast it from thee: it is better for thee to enter into life with one eye, rather than having two eyes to be cast into hell fire. (Matthew 18:8–9)

> Then shall he say also unto them on the left hand, Depart from me, ye cursed, into everlasting fire, prepared for the devil and his angels. (Matthew 25:41)

> And these shall go away into everlasting punishment: but the righteous into life eternal. (Matthew 25:46)

> And if thy hand offend thee, cut it off: it is better for thee to enter into life maimed, than having two hands to go into hell, into the fire that never shall be quenched: where their worm dieth not, and the fire is not quenched. And if thy foot offend thee, cut it off: it is better for thee to enter halt into life, than having two feet to be cast into

hell, into the fire that never shall be quenched: where their worm dieth not, and the fire is not quenched. And if thine eye offend thee, pluck it out: it is better for thee to enter into the kingdom of God with one eye, than having two eyes to be cast into hell fire: where their worm dieth not, and the fire is not quenched. (Mark 9:43–48)

Clearly, these texts, which superficially conflict with the great testimony of Scripture, must be addressed.

Further, John in Revelation uses the term *ever and ever* in relation to the final punishment of the wicked.

And the smoke of their torment ascendeth up for ever and ever: and they have no rest day nor night, who worship the beast and his image, and whosoever receiveth the mark of his name. (Revelation 14:11)

And the devil that deceived them was cast into the lake of fire and brimstone, where the beast and the false prophet are, and shall be tormented day and night for ever and ever. (Revelation 20:10)

Do these texts of Scripture provide evidence that God's Word is unreliable and supports a plurality of views on this vital doctrine? Certainly not! God is not a source of pluralism. He speaks but truth.

Let us first examine the expressions of eternity used in the book of Matthew. The English language has no precise word for the Greek word *aionios* from which the terms *everlasting, eternal,* and *for ever* are translated. The emphasis in the word is that the action described will last until it is completed and no act will halt it before that time. When this fact is appreciated, then these texts present no problem and are perfectly compatible with the mass of Scripture as it enlightens the reader concerning the state of the dead.

Speaking of the use of the word "forever" in the third angels' message of Revelation 14:9–11, the word *aion*, here translated "forever," is defined thus by G. Abbot-Smith in *A Manual Greek Lexicon of the New Testament:*

> A space of time, as, a lifetime, generation, period of history, an indefinitely long period.

We would illustrate this use of the word *eternal*:

> Even as Sodom and Gomorrha, and the cities about them in like manner, giving themselves over to fornication, and going after strange flesh, are set forth for an example, suffering the vengeance of eternal fire. (Jude 1:7)

The cities of Sodom and Gomorrha were situated near the Dead Sea. There is now no continuous fire there. Thus the "eternal" fire mentioned by Jude had been extinguished for almost two thousand years at the time this epistle was written. The fire was "eternal" in the sense that it did not abate until its entire work of destruction of the cities was accomplished. Further, it cannot be denied that the fire had eternal consequences. In 1981, Colin visited the region where Sodom was located. Of course, he saw no sign of a continuously burning fire.

Similarly, the fire which destroys the wicked also burns until sinners are no more, and it, too, will have eternal consequences—eternal destruction of the wicked. In his preaching, John the Baptist confirmed this fact when he preached that God will burn up the chaff with unquenchable fire. (See Matthew 3:12)

It is true that the same Greek word *aionios* is used to describe the eternal life awarded to the righteous. In view of the foregoing could this word usage take away our certainty of real life? Could it be that our reward is only for a certain period? No! The Bible clearly states that there will be no death in the New Earth:

> And God shall wipe away all tears from their eyes; and there shall be no more death, neither sorrow, nor crying,

neither shall there be any more pain: for the former things are passed away. (Revelation 21:4)

Neither can they die any more: for they are equal unto the angels; and are the children of God, being the children of the resurrection. (Luke 20:36)

Thus *aionios*, literally "lasting for an age" means, when related to the righteous, an age which is eternal. In contrast the Bible plainly states that the reward of the wicked is eternal destruction.

And to you who are troubled rest with us, when the Lord Jesus shall be revealed from heaven with his mighty angels, in flaming fire taking vengeance on them that know not God, and that obey not the gospel of our Lord Jesus Christ: who shall be punished with everlasting destruction from the presence of the Lord, and from the glory of his power. (2 Thessalonians 1:7–9)

Thus we can fully understand the words of Jesus,

And these shall go away into everlasting punishment: but the righteous into life eternal. (Matthew 25:46)

It is plain that when Jesus speaks of "everlasting punishment," He is declaring that the punishment, which is destruction, is everlasting. There is no further opportunity to live again.

Now let us turn to the puzzling statement of Jesus as recorded in Mark. As cited above, Jesus referred to "the fire that shall never be quenched" and the "worm that dieth not." Some attempt to equate this worm with the soul and thus set this passage forth as evidence of eternal punishment. But there is not the least evidence that the "worm" here referred to is a synonym for the soul.

The meaning of Jesus becomes far clearer when we recognize that He is quoting from the Old Testament. Let us examine the relevant verse:

> And they shall go forth, and look upon the carcases of
> the men that have transgressed against me: for their worm
> shall not die, neither shall their fire be quenched; and they
> shall be an abhorring unto all flesh. (Isaiah 66:24)

". . .worm shall not die." In this text it will be seen that the redeemed
are viewing dead carcasses, or as some translations have used, corpses;
not living souls. In this context it is obvious that this reference to worms
does not refer to some spark of life that is in these corpses. Obviously,
if they were carcasses or corpses, the spirit would have already left and
would be somewhere else, so the meaning of this difficult text cannot sus-
tain immediate life after death—especially in the light of the many other
evidences in the Bible that death is devoid of consciousness. The Hebrew
verb translated "die" is expressed in the simple-imperfect tense, which
denotes incomplete action rather than an eternal reality. Thus the Bible
records, using the simple-imperfect tense, that Adam and Eve were not
ashamed of their nakedness in the Garden of Eden (Genesis 2:25). That
this did not refer to an everlasting situation is proven by the fact that they
later became very ashamed of their condition of nakedness (Genesis 3:7).
The simple-imperfect tense denotes a temporary condition. Thus these
worms most certainly will be destroyed in the unquenchable fires.

But does this term "unquenchable" refer to everlasting hell fire? As
we examine this matter, it is well to note that John the Baptist also spoke
of such a fire.

> I indeed baptize you with water unto repentance: but
> he that cometh after me is mightier than I, whose shoes I
> am not worthy to bear: he shall baptize you with the Holy
> Ghost, and with fire: whose fan is in his hand, and he will
> throughly purge his floor, and gather his wheat into the
> garner; but he will burn up the chaff with unquenchable
> fire. (Matthew 3:11–12)

Once again the Greek word from which "unquenchable" is translated
is in the simple-imperfect tense and thus this passage simply means that

the fire cannot be extinguished before it completes its work of burning up the wicked.

That this is the correct meaning of this word may be seen from the fact that God predicted that an unquenchable fire would be sent upon Jerusalem.

> But if ye will not hearken unto me to hallow the sabbath day, and not to bear a burden, even entering in at the gates of Jerusalem on the sabbath day; then will I kindle a fire in the gates thereof, and it shall devour the palaces of Jerusalem, and it shall not be quenched. (Jeremiah 17:27)

That prophecy was fulfilled, no man could put the fire out, and Jerusalem was destroyed by fire.

> And they burnt the house of God, and brake down the wall of Jerusalem, and burnt all the palaces thereof with fire, and destroyed all the goodly vessels thereof. (2 Chronicles 36:19)

Although the city was burned by the Babylonians, that fire eventually ceased.

So it may be seen that Jesus' use of Isaiah as recorded in Mark 9 referred merely to the destruction of the wicked.

In Revelation 14:11 it is stated that "the smoke of their torment ascendeth for ever and ever." Once again an Old-Testament expression has been borrowed:

> It shall not be quenched night nor day; the smoke thereof shall go up for ever: from generation to generation it shall lie waste; none shall pass through it for ever and ever. (Isaiah 34:10)

This verse refers to the destruction of Idumea (Edom) (see Isaiah 34:5, 6). No one would suggest that the smoke of Edom (the land of the descendants of Esau) has risen for eternity. As has been noted, this statement simply refers to the inevitability of the completion of the destruction. So, too, it will be with the punishment of the unrepentant.

It is only as we compare Scripture with Scripture and also understand the usage of the word in the original language that we can understand that Scripture is entirely consistent and not contradictory. Even today, when a young man promises his girlfriend that he will love her for ever, he is understood to limit this love to his lifetime. This, too, was true of Hannah's vow to take Samuel to the tabernacle so that he could dwell there "for ever."

> But Hannah went not up; for she said unto her husband, I will not go up until the child be weaned, and then I will bring him, that he may appear before the LORD, and there abide *for ever*. (1 Samuel 1:22)

That this vow simply implied the desire of Hannah that Samuel should dwell there until his death is confirmed in this scriptural passage:

> Therefore also I have lent him to the LORD; *as long as he liveth* he shall be lent to the LORD. And he worshipped the LORD there. (1 Samuel 1:28)

Also before her statement in 1 Samuel 1:22, she had made the intent of this comment plain.

> And she vowed a vow, and said, O LORD of hosts, if thou wilt indeed look on the affliction of thine handmaid, and remember me, and not forget thine handmaid, but wilt give unto thine handmaid a man child, then I will give him unto the LORD *all the days of his life*, and there shall no razor come upon his head. (1 Samuel 1:11)

CHAPTER 11

Our Father in a World of Terrorism

D URING the Vietnam War, Colin was chairman of the educational department at Avondale College in New South Wales, Australia. The French teacher at the college, John Reynaud , the son of a French farmer, had been born in Hanoi. He had joined the French Army in defending the French colonial government against the uprising in Indo-China (Vietnam, Cambodia, and Laos) in the 1950s. In 1965, this man told Colin that it was impossible for the Americans to win the war against Vietnam. Colin was skeptical of this evaluation. But Mr. Reynaud was adamant.

Six months before the French capitulated to the Indo-Chinese people, the commander of the French forces had confidently predicted victory in the conflict within the next six months. Colin's colleague explained that the Indo-Chinese had been fighting wars constantly for more than two hundred years, and they knew that the Westerners could not endure a long war. He further explained the Indo-Chinese strategy. They would mount a big offensive, and the French military would concentrate their forces to fight it. When the French forces were concentrated in one location, the Indo-Chinese would open up many small offensives, and the French had to hasten to the countryside to meet these many challenges. Then the strategy would be repeated. As Colin followed the Vietnam War, he saw the same strategy employed against the allied forces. The Americans and their allies were unable to develop a strategy to counter these Vietnamese initiatives.

In May 1968, Russell took the short flight from Phnom Penh, Cambodia, to Saigon, South Vietnam. The purpose of this visit was to attend a Medical Convention held at the United States' Ninety-Third Evacuation Hospital in Long Binh Province. As the plane came in to land, Russell was not a little disconcerted to observe numerous bomb craters in the vicinity of the airport. Upon alighting from the aircraft, he found that half the terminal had been destroyed by terrorists, as he travelled to Long Binh, he discovered that the large bridge crossing the Mekong River had its left-hand section destroyed by terrorist activity the previous week.

In 1968, Saigon was akin to Baghdad in 2006, and the Vietnamese countryside was as dangerous as Iraq as we write. Three months earlier, in February 1968, the fearful Tet (Vietnamese New Year) Offensive had proved to be a turning point in the war. At the American Military Hospital in Long Binh, Russell observed first-hand the fearful toll upon the American Army by a foe elusive and effective against a vastly superior military force. Helicopters, in rapid succession, landed with fearfully wounded soldiers, many having stepped upon land mines.

By 1974, the terrorist forces of the South Vietnamese Viet Cong, as much feared then as al-Qa'ida is in the twenty-first century, had won the war, and the Americans and their allies evacuated their forces, leaving the country united under the Communist government the West had attempted to destroy.

Russell visited the mighty armament stockpiles in Saigon and marveled that the Western nations were impotent to succeed in this war on terrorism against a nation of such inferior military might. The power of the terrorist was entrenched from that time on.

Russell almost lost his life to such terrorism when he was travelling with his father (Darcy Standish), an American orthodontist, and an American physician and their families in a "safe" region of Laos, only twenty-five miles (forty kilometers) north of Vientiane, the capital city. Upon turning a corner on a road, they were confronted by a road block manned by eleven Pathet Lao insurgents (Laotian Communist guerrillas). The leader of the group, a man of fierce visage, placed the barrel of his rifle on the orthodontist's temple and demanded, in poor English, to see his passport. Naturally this man, Dr. Art Ewart, was so disquieted by this perilous situation that he could scarcely enunciate any words as he tried to explain the fact that he had not brought his or his family's passports with him. Praise God he had not! This oversight was to prove, under God's grace, the group's salvation.

As the leader spoke with increasingly violent demands for that which the orthodontist could not produce, Russell, who had his father's and his own passports in his pocket, called out, "I've got passports." Immediately the leading terrorist took his rifle from the orthodontist's temple and pressed the barrel of his rifle into Russell's. Russell did not know if he had another millionth second of life. We do not have to convince each reader that our silent prayers to God at that moment for His rescue possessed no atom of insincerity!

Russell thrust the two passports into the hand of the insurgent leader. He looked down at the passports momentarily and then looked up in surprise, "You Australia?" he asked. Russell confirmed the fact. Then came beautiful words—"Australia all right." These rebels knew their politics. They were searching for Americans, for the United States was attempting, again unsuccessfully, to quell this terrorist uprising. Australia had participated in the Vietnam War, but in 1972, the new Australian government of Mr. Gough Whitlam had withdrawn all Australian troops from the region. Of course, our father and Russell had no say in this government reversal, but we surely benefited, under God's protecting hand, from it.

The leading terrorist assumed that all passengers in the minibus were Australians and released us. How we thank God that the orthodontist had left his passport in the capital city. Had he possessed it, it is almost certain that all occupants of the vehicle would have lost their lives.

We often hear Christians perplexed by the Almighty God's failing to interfere in wanton acts of terrorism. Such questions were asked after the massive death toll in the Twin Towers in New York and the Pentagon on September 11, 2001. How do such acts measure up to the biblical assertions that God is both omnipotent and He is love? Could God prevent the current age of terrorism? Could He cure every cancer victim? Could He not prevent every motor vehicle accident? Of course, He could! Then why does He not do so?

This is a question which has tortured the minds of faithful believers, no doubt since the entry of sin into our earth. Why did He save Russell and our father and travelling companions and not others in similar dire circumstances? Russell and our father were not saved by God for any virtue they possessed. Of that fact we are absolutely certain. But we are equally certain that it was not just "luck" on our part. Our dear father now rests in the grave.[1] He was a God-fearing man. God provided him twenty-three further years of life. We are prepared to await the answer to God's protection on that day when we sit at Christ's feet in His kingdom. One matter remains. We continue to thank Him from the depths of our hearts for His protection on that and many other occasions when our lives were in peril.

This question is a most perplexing issue, as are other matters akin to it. When Pope Benedict XVI visited the former Nazi German concentration camp, Auschwitz, located in Poland, in early June, 2006, he posed similar questions,

> Where was God in those days? Why was He silent?
> How could He permit this senseless slaughter, this triumph
> of evil? (*The Boston Globe*, [U.S.A.] June 4, 2006)

We are poor humans with little wisdom. We are not able to solve every matter inferred in the question of why God does not prevent every act of barbarism perpetrated in this old world. But we have sought to study, as best we can, praying for the Holy Spirit's guidance, God's rescuing plan of salvation. When we ponder the infinite price paid by God's Son for our salvation and recognize that the whole of heaven was bankrupted during Christ's earthly life, we do not for a single moment doubt our heavenly Father's love and wisdom.

We have been impressed by some of the insights of the nineteenth-century biblical expositor we have quoted earlier in this book. But first let us find clues to this apparent conundrum in Scripture.

> How art thou fallen from heaven, O Lucifer, son of
> the morning! how art thou cut down to the ground, which
> didst weaken the nations! For thou hast said in thine heart,
> I will ascend into heaven, I will exalt my throne above the
> stars of God: I will sit also upon the mount of the congre-

---

1. Russell also now rests in the grave, these five volumes being some of the last manuscripts he was preparing for publication before his tragic death in an automobile collision.

gation, in the sides of the north: I will ascend above the heights of the clouds; I will be like the most High. (Isaiah 14:12–14)

For the first time in the history of eternity a created being, Lucifer, the "anointed cherub that covereth" (Ezekiel 28:14), aspired to be as God, a rank that was neither accorded him nor was it possible to achieve. There will always remain an infinite "chasm" between the Everlasting Creator and all of His creatures. That Lucifer did not keep his unsanctified ambitions to himself is plain from the fact that one-third of the angelic host were beguiled by Lucifer's claims.

> And there was war in heaven: Michael [Christ] and his angels fought against the dragon; and the dragon fought and his angels, and prevailed not; neither was their place found any more in heaven. And the great dragon was cast out, that old serpent, called the Devil, and Satan, which deceiveth the whole world: he was cast out into the earth, and his angels were cast out with him. (Revelation 12:7–9)

> And his [Satan's] tail drew the third part of the stars [angels] of heaven, and did cast them to the earth. . . . (Revelation 12:4)

From the eons of eternity pure love and harmony was found in the universe. Unquestionably every angel, including Lucifer, possessed perfect peace and happiness in their service to God. How the previously unknown thought of rebellion arose in Lucifer's heart will ever remain a mystery. Certainly there was no tempter to tempt him. In fact, as we ponder this matter, it is clear in our minds that if there was discovered a valid cause to provoke Lucifer's first stirrings of sin, this would provide an excuse for his actions. But sin is never excusable, much as we humans often futilely attempt to excuse the inexcusable in our own lives. It is a deliberate decision on our part to disobey God.

We can scarcely imagine the subtlety by which Lucifer pressed his rebellious concepts upon his fellow angels. No doubt his post as the covering cherub, the one who stood by God's throne and was close to Him in His counsels, provided Lucifer with credibility with the lower ranked angels. Further, the Bible states,

> Thine heart was lifted up because of thy beauty, thou hast corrupted thy wisdom by reason of thy brightness. . . . (Ezekiel 28:17)

It is manifest that Lucifer was the most beautiful, the wisest, and possessed the greatest physical glory of all the created beings. No doubt, the remainder of the angels were ever willing to undertake the covering cherub's biddings. Scripture provides no inkling of how long Lucifer had lived before sin held fast in his mind. We will inquire of this matter as we sit at our Master's feet, learning ever more of the origin of sin and the infinite plan of salvation. But for now, we will not speculate, and we will patiently await to ask this and numerous other questions of our Saviour at that glorious time.

In harmony with evidence from Scripture, Mrs. White stated,

> In heaven itself this law was broken. Sin originated in self-seeking. Lucifer, the covering cherub, desired to be first in heaven. He sought to gain control of heavenly beings, to draw them away from their Creator, and to win their homage to himself. Therefore he misrepresented God, attributing to Him the desire for self-exaltation. With his own evil characteristics he sought to invest the loving Creator. Thus he deceived angels. (*The Desire of Ages*, pp. 21, 22)

We know how successful Satan has been in destroying the basis of the government of God—His law—among professing Christians. Many today take the illogical position that the Ten Commandments were abolished at the cross and that we are now under grace and not law.

The very presence of God's grace is evidence beyond all doubt that the holy law of God is still the basis of God's eternal kingdom. Our need of grace presupposes a persisting holy law. If there is no law to breach there is no sin,

> . . . for sin is the transgression of the law. (1 John 3:4)

If there was no law of God, there would be no sin, just as if there was no law against excessive speeds on the road, one could drive through a suburban street at 187 miles (300 kilometers) per hour without fear of penalty, for no law would have been broken. Compelling evidence that the Ten Commandments still prevail is found in words written over six decades after Christ's death, defining God's last-day saints:

> Here is the patience of the saints: here are they that
> keep the commandments of God, and the faith of Jesus.
> (Revelation 14:12)

This passage would possess no meaning if the Ten Commandment Law was annulled at the cross. Many other New-Testament texts confirm the perpetuity of the law. (See Revelation 12:17; 22:14; 1 John 2:3–6; 1 John 3:3–9; Ephesians 6:2; 1 Corinthians 7:19.)

Since Satan has assiduously sought to destroy God's law in the Christian Church, it is likely that, as he does today, he presented it as a matter of bondage to the angels. All committed Christians love God's law, for they love God.

> By this we know that we love the children of God,
> when we love God, and keep his commandments. For this
> is the love of God, that we keep his commandments: and
> his commandments are not grievous. (1 John 5:2–3)

Of course, God's commandments are wholly grievous to those who wish to disobey God. Clearly, this became the tenor of Lucifer's thoughts. This view he sought to implant in the minds of angels.

Unquestionably we are saved by God's grace alone and not by our keeping of God's Commandments. Paul made this matter clear.

> For by grace are ye saved through faith; and that not of yourselves: it is the gift of God: Not of works, lest any man should boast. (Ephesians 2:8–9)

But obedience to God's law, under the indwelling power of the Holy Spirit, is a condition of God for the bestowing of His grace. The following verse states:

> For we are his workmanship, created in Christ Jesus unto good works, which God hath before ordained that we should walk in them. (Ephesians 2:10)

God cannot bestow His heavenly grace upon those humans, whatever their profession, who would bring to heaven with them the same sin of rebellion which excluded Satan and his angelic followers from heaven. The peace of the universe would ever remain blighted if God chose such a course. If we are not righteous and wholly relying upon God's power to live such sanctified lives (see Revelation 22:14), He will not, at His second coming, make us into robots, forcing us to keep the peace of heaven. The very fact that sin did enter the universe is proof positive that God grants His created beings free choice.

Let us return to our question, Why does God not foil all acts of terrorism and crime? Let us again remember that the nature and consequences of sin were not known among the angels, nor by created beings on other planets scattered throughout the universe.

These created beings possessed no knowledge of whether Lucifer's claims of a superior concept of order in the universe were correct or false. They had never known adverse emotions such as hatred, fear, jealousy, unholy ambitions, wrath, selfishness, pride, and a host of other sinful emotions. Because these are fully revealed to our earthly minds today, provides us with an advantage. But if God had chosen to subvert every proposed act of evil, we would not have been in a position to discern between God's love and Satan's hatred. Satan's course had to be permitted to be revealed to holy angels, humans and other created sentient beings. Only thus could the evil of sin be eradicated once and for all from God's kingdom. To have prevented the eruption of fearful, sinful acts would not have been an act of infinite love, but, rather, a cover-up which would ever have left God's created children vulnerable to evil. This fact has been well expressed.

> His [Satan's] power to deceive was very great. By disguising himself in a cloak of falsehood, he had gained an advantage. All his acts were so clothed with mystery that it was difficult to disclose to the angels the true nature of his work. Until fully developed, it could not be made to appear the evil thing it was; his disaffection would not be seen to be rebellion. Even the loyal angels could not fully discern his character or see to what his work was leading. (E. G. White, *Patriarchs and Prophets*, p. 41)

Further, Ellen White, with great perception wrote:

> God could employ only such means as were consistent with truth and righteousness. Satan could use what God could not—flattery and deceit. He had sought to falsify the word of God and had misrepresented His plan of government, claiming that God was not just in imposing laws upon the angels; that in requiring submission and obedience from His creatures, He was seeking merely the exaltation of Himself. It was therefore necessary to demonstrate before the inhabitants of heaven, and of all the worlds, that God's government is just, His law perfect. Satan had made it appear that he himself was seeking to promote the good of the universe. The true character of the usurper and his real object must be understood by all. He must have time to manifest himself by his wicked works. (*Ibid*, p. 42)

So why did God not annihilate Satan and his angelic host?

> Even when he was cast out of heaven, Infinite Wisdom did not destroy Satan. Since only the service of love can be acceptable to God, the allegiance of His creatures must rest upon a conviction of His justice and benevolence. The inhabitants of heaven and of the worlds, being unprepared to comprehend the nature or consequences of sin, could not then have seen the justice of God in the destruction of Satan. Had he been immediately blotted out of existence, some would have served God from fear rather than from love. The influence of the deceiver would not have been fully destroyed, nor would the spirit of rebellion have been utterly eradicated. For the good of the entire universe through ceaseless ages, he must more fully develop his principles, that his charges against the divine government might be seen in their true light by all created beings, and that the justice and mercy of God and the immutability of His law might be forever placed beyond all question. (Ibid.)

Let us catch a glimpse of the wisdom of God in the fate of one holy prophet, John the Baptist. Many question why Christ permitted his execution at the hands of King Herod when He could so easily have rescued him from his dungeon. Past years have raised up not a few excellent biblical expositors. However, we have found Ellen White to have exceeded them in the breadth of Scripture she brings to bear on matters of great difficulty, such as the issue of John the Baptist's death and its relationship to the horrors transpiring in our world. We quote a little from her insights on this matter.[1]

---

1. So outstanding is Ellen White's biography of Christ in His earthly life that we are offering this book to the reader at a reasonable price. Please write to Remnant Herald, P.O. Box 175, Kalorama, Victoria, 3766, Australia or Fax 03-97511648 or e-mail remnantherald@optusnet.com.au or phone 03-97511932. In the phone and fax numbers for overseas calls please drop the zero and dial 011-613-9751-1932. Please request the book *The Desire of Ages*. You may also request this book from Hartland Publications.

Why did God not spare John the Baptist's young life? He was only six months older than Christ and about thirty-two years old when he was beheaded. Mrs. White's answer exceeds any we could suggest.

> Jesus did not interpose to deliver His servant. He knew that John would bear the test. Gladly would the Saviour have come to John, to brighten the dungeon gloom with His own presence. But He was not to place Himself in the hands of enemies and imperil His own mission. Gladly would He have delivered His faithful servant. But for the sake of thousands who in after years must pass from prison to death, John was to drink the cup of martyrdom. As the followers of Jesus should languish in lonely cells, or perish by the sword, the rack, or the fagot, apparently forsaken by God and man, what a stay to their hearts would be the thought that John the Baptist, to whose faithfulness Christ Himself had borne witness, had passed through a similar experience!
>
> Satan was permitted to cut short the earthly life of God's messenger; but that life which "is hid with Christ in God," the destroyer could not reach. Colossians 3:3. He exulted that he had brought sorrow upon Christ, but he had failed of conquering John. Death itself only placed him forever beyond the power of temptation. In this warfare, Satan was revealing his own character. Before the witnessing universe he made manifest his enmity toward God and man. (*The Desire of Ages*, p. 224)

A further matter is also elucidated:

> God never leads His children otherwise than they would choose to be led, if they could see the end from the beginning, and discern the glory of the purpose which they are fulfilling as co-workers with Him. Not Enoch, who was translated to heaven, not Elijah, who ascended in a chariot of fire, was greater or more honored than John

the Baptist, who perished alone in the dungeon. "Unto you it is given in the behalf of Christ, not only to believe on Him, but also to suffer for His sake." Philippians 1:29. And of all the gifts that Heaven can bestow upon men, fellowship with Christ in His sufferings is the most weighty trust and the highest honor. (Ibid, pp. 224-225)

We, among many other Christians, have often wondered whether John the Baptist was raised from the dead about two years later, at the time of Christ's resurrection. That many saints were resurrected at this time Scripture attests:

And the graves were opened; and many bodies of the saints which slept arose, and came out of the graves after his resurrection, and went into the holy city, and appeared unto many. (Matthew 27:52–53)

This event fulfilled the ancient prophecy of Isaiah:

Thy dead men shall live, together with my dead body shall they arise. Awake and sing, ye that dwell in dust: for thy dew is as the dew of herbs, and the earth shall cast out the dead. (Isaiah 26:19)

In heaven we will discover whether John the Baptist is in heaven now or whether he is awaiting the glorious resurrection just prior to the Second Coming, as are the faithful of all ages.

The current world racked with acts of terrorism in many countries and other revolting crimes shouts in our ears that the second coming of Christ is near at hand. What a time to be ready! This is a time to separate from worldly lusts and seek God's empowering grace and His tender love. Remember that He has exhorted us,

For even hereunto were ye called: because Christ also suffered for us, leaving us an example, that ye should follow his steps: who did no sin, neither was guile found in his mouth. (1 Peter 2:21–22)

We conclude with one further insight from our biblical favorite expositor:

> He that ruleth in the heavens is the one who sees the end from the beginning—the one before whom the mysteries of the past and the future are alike outspread, and who, beyond the woe and darkness and ruin that sin has wrought, beholds the accomplishment of His own purposes of love and blessing. Though "clouds and darkness are round about Him: righteousness and judgment are the foundation of His throne." Psalm 97:2, R.V. And this the inhabitants of the universe, both loyal and disloyal, will one day understand. "His work is perfect: for all His ways are judgment: a God of truth and without iniquity, just and right is He." Deuteronomy 32:4. (*Patriarchs and Prophets*, p. 43)

God's justice and His love will then be fully revealed:

> And they sing the song of Moses the servant of God, and the song of the Lamb, saying, Great and marvellous are thy works, Lord God Almighty; just and true are thy ways, thou King of saints. (Revelation 15:3)

Even the lost, as they stand before God's judgment throne, also admit God's justice. Thus the annuls of the universe will ever testify that every created being, unfallen, fallen but redeemed, and lost, will have testified to God's love and His scrupulously impartial justice.

> Who shall not fear thee, O Lord, and glorify thy name? for thou only art holy: for all nations shall come and worship before thee; for thy judgments are made manifest. (Revelation 15:4)

Only then will those who have rejected Christ's salvation, so dearly purchased, be forever destroyed.

> And I saw a great white throne, and him that sat on it, from whose face the earth and the heaven fled away; and there was found no place for them. And I saw the dead, small and great, stand before God; and the books were opened: and another book was opened, which is the book of life: and the dead were judged out of those things which were written in the books, according to their works. And the sea gave up the dead which were in it; and death and hell delivered up the dead which were in them: and they were judged every man according to their works. And death and hell were cast into the lake of fire. This is the second death. (Revelation 20:11–14)

Despite the horrifying acts of terrorism today, God is still holding back the great majority of Satan's evil designs. Once His four angels who hold back the winds of strife complete their duty just prior to the pouring out of the last seven plagues, we shall be able then to discern just how much our loving God has intervened on mankind's behalf, only permitting Satan to undertake that small proportion of his vile designs against mankind, as will provide us sufficient evidence of his evil character.

> And after these things I saw four angels standing on the four corners of the earth, holding the four winds of the earth, that the wind should not blow on the earth, nor on the sea, nor on any tree. And I saw another angel ascending from the east, having the seal of the living God: and he cried with a loud voice to the four angels, to whom it was given to hurt the earth and the sea, saying, Hurt not the earth, neither the sea, nor the trees, till we have sealed the servants of our God in their foreheads. (Revelation 7:1–3)

With the completion of God's judgment, the redeemed finally separated from those who have chosen to reject God's blessed offer of salvation, then will be seen the full measure of Satan's designs against humanity.

> And at that time shall Michael stand up, the great prince which standeth for the children of thy people: and there shall be a time of trouble, such as never was since there was a nation even to that same time: and at that time thy people shall be delivered, every one that shall be found written in the book. (Daniel 12:1)

We thank God that His living redeemed, although still upon this earth, will be protected from the plagues and death. (See our book, *The Rapture, the End-Time and the Millennium.*) This assurance God provided for His true followers, using wonderful poetic imagery.

> He that dwelleth in the secret place of the most High shall abide under the shadow of the Almighty. I will say of the Lord, He is my refuge and my fortress: my God; in him will I trust. Surely he shall deliver thee from the snare of the fowler, and from the noisome pestilence. He shall cover thee with his feathers, and under his wings shalt thou trust: his truth shall be thy shield and buckler. Thou shalt not be afraid for the terror by night; nor for the arrow that flieth by day; nor for the pestilence that walketh in darkness; nor for the destruction that wasteth at noonday. A thousand shall fall at thy side, and ten thousand at thy right hand; but it shall not come nigh thee. Only with thine eyes shalt thou behold and see the reward of the wicked. Because thou hast made the Lord, which is my refuge, even the most High, thy habitation; there shall no evil befall thee, neither shall any plague come nigh thy dwelling. For he shall give his angels charge over thee, to keep thee in all thy ways. They shall bear thee up in their hands, lest thou dash thy foot against a stone. (Psalm 91:1–12)

CHAPTER 12

Our Wonderful Father

WHEN we see our Father in His true character we will sing an ancient Hebrew hymn from the depths of our hearts with the psalmist:

> O give thanks unto the LORD; call upon his name: make known his deeds among the people. Sing unto him, sing psalms unto him: talk ye of all his wondrous works. Glory ye in his holy name: let the heart of them rejoice that seek the LORD. Seek the LORD, and his strength: seek his face evermore. Remember his marvellous works that he hath done; his wonders, and the judgments of his mouth. (Psalm 105:1–5)

If Christians would spend more time in extolling the name of God, we would draw so much closer to Him and never doubt His magnanimous and undeserved love toward us. Too often, we wallow in doubt and despair when we should be seeking our Father while basking confidently with great gratitude in His love. There was wise counsel provided in a hymn we used to sing as lads. It commenced,

> When upon life's billows you are tempest tossed,
> When you are discouraged thinking all is lost,
> Count your many blessings, name them one by one,
> And it will surprise you what the Lord hath done.

Frequently we spend much more time counting our woes and spare little time to thank God for every day of life He has granted us, food on the table every day, water, clothing, shelter, and the presence by our sides of loved ones.

On the 15th of August, 1995, we surprised one another when in a telephone call, without ever a single word of prior discussion, we found that each of us was "celebrating" a very unusual anniversary. We had just reached 61 years and 193 days of life. Maybe no other human being had ever celebrated this "birthday." But it was of great significance to us. That was the age of our wonderful, and dear mother, Hilda Marie Joyce Standish, nee Bailey, when she died of a heart attack on May 5, 1974. Every day of our lives since that day has been appreciated as a great gift of life from God. Even now we still miss our mother as we do our father, Darcy Rowland Standish (1912–1997), whom God blessed with over twenty-three years more life than our mother. The privilege of being born into a dedicated Christian home is a blessing for which we ever thank our God.

But infinitely beyond our dear parents' love for us is the love of our Father in Heaven. He is the One

> In whom are hid all the treasures of wisdom and knowledge. (Colossians 2:3)

No human parent can begin to match such wisdom and knowledge. The word "treasures" in this passage of Scripture possesses a depth of meaning which will attract our understanding for eternity. Notice the words of the previous verse which describes these treasures as a mystery to our feeble mortal minds:

> That their hearts might be comforted, being knit together in love, and unto all riches of the full assurance of understanding, to the acknowledgement of the mystery of God, and of the Father, and of Christ. (Colossians 2:2)

But, nevertheless, there is an assurance provided of understanding. It is a mystery, the details of which slowly unravel as, in the Father's love, we contemplate His Word. We must accept the fact that it is only as we yield our lives to God through sincere prayer and the study of His Word that we can grow in this understanding and increase in confidence in His Word.

> Because the carnal mind is enmity against God: for it is not subject to the law of God, neither indeed can be. So then they that are in the flesh cannot please God. (Romans 8:7–8)

In this passage of the Bible, the word "flesh" is not referring to the flesh of our bodies. This is plainly evident from the following verse, written to believers in the city of Rome who were well and truly alive.

> But ye are not in the flesh, but in the Spirit, if so be that the Spirit of God dwell in you. Now if any man have not the Spirit of Christ, he is none of his. And if Christ be in you, the body is dead because of sin; but the Spirit is life because of righteousness. But if the Spirit of him that raised up Jesus from the dead dwell in you, he that raised up Christ from the dead shall also quicken your mortal bodies by his Spirit that dwelleth in you. Therefore, brethren, we are debtors, not to the flesh, to live after the flesh. For if ye live after the flesh, ye shall die: but if ye through the Spirit do mortify the deeds of the body, ye shall live. For as many as are led by the Spirit of God, they are the sons of God. (Romans 8:9–14)

We suggest these words be re-read and pondered. It is good to meditate upon God's Word, under the guidance of the Holy Spirit. Have you noticed the final words of this promise—"sons of God"? Are we really sons of God? If we accept Christ as our Saviour, the Father elevates us to sons and daughters of Him! On this matter our Father's Word is explicit. Speaking of those who, in the strength of the Holy Spirit, turn their hearts to God, we are promised,

> Wherefore come out from among them, and be ye
> separate, saith the Lord, and touch not the unclean thing;
> and I will receive you, and will be a Father unto you,
> and ye shall be my sons and daughters, saith the Lord
> Almighty. (2 Corinthians 6:17–18)

Contrary to the teaching of some religions which misunderstand God's tender love for women, God desires for our dear ladies to be princesses of His kingdom. While God ascribes different roles to men and women, nevertheless, there is full equality of status. God promises to both men and women the privilege of being His heirs on the same terms:

> Likewise, ye husbands, dwell with them according
> to knowledge, giving honour unto the wife, as unto the
> weaker vessel, and as being heirs together of the grace of
> life; that your prayers be not hindered. (1 Peter 3:7)

In the Old-Testament era our Father revealed Himself to Israel in words of tenderness:

> And the Lord passed by before him, and proclaimed, The
> Lord, The Lord God, merciful and gracious, longsuffering,
> and abundant in goodness and truth, keeping mercy for thou-
> sands, forgiving iniquity and transgression and sin, and that
> will by no means clear the guilty; visiting the iniquity of the
> fathers upon the children, and upon the children's children,
> unto the third and to the fourth generation. (Exodus 34:6–7)

We can daily claim this divine revelation. Those who seek to set forth the Father as a fierce tyrant in contrast to the Son as one of gracious pity and love, do the Father a gross injustice. The ancient prophets knew no such heavenly Father. Jonah knew the mercy of His God.

> And he prayed unto the Lord, and said, I pray thee, O
> Lord, was not this my saying, when I was yet in my coun-

try? Therefore I fled before unto Tarshish: for I knew that thou art a gracious God, and merciful, slow to anger, and of great kindness, and repentest thee of the evil. (Jonah 4:2)

Jonah lived in the ninth century BC. Micah, another prophet living in the following century, was full of understanding of His God, as expressed in the concluding words of his prophecy:

> Who is a God like unto thee, that pardoneth iniquity, and passeth by the transgression of the remnant of his heritage? he retaineth not his anger for ever, because he delighteth in mercy. He will turn again, he will have compassion upon us; he will subdue our iniquities; and thou wilt cast all their sins into the depths of the sea. Thou wilt perform the truth to Jacob, and the mercy to Abraham, which thou hast sworn unto our fathers from the days of old. (Micah 7:18–20)

Many Christians overlook the part played by God in the plan of salvation. Inspired by the Holy Spirit, Paul the Apostle was in no doubt concerning this matter:

> And all things are of God, who hath reconciled us to himself by Jesus Christ, and hath given to us the ministry of reconciliation; to wit, that God was in Christ, reconciling the world unto himself, not imputing their trespasses unto them; and hath committed unto us the word of reconciliation. Now then we are ambassadors for Christ, as though God did beseech you by us: we pray you in Christ's stead, be ye reconciled to God. For he hath made him to be sin for us, who knew no sin; that we might be made the righteousness of God in him. (2 Corinthians 5:18–21)

We can never overstate Christ's sufferings for us. But often we greatly underestimate the Father's sufferings. Yet a reflection upon our human emotions, if we had to endure the torture of a much-loved son before our eyes, would provide a minimal glimpse of the agony it was for the infinite Father to stand by and behold the treatment, beyond all torture, meted out to His beloved Son. Even worse, our omniscient God had to anticipate this event from eternity. Further, God possessed such power that in a moment of time He could have rescued His Son from His terrible ordeal. When we contemplate this fact, we will never doubt God's love for us. In Christ's agony in the Garden of Gethsemane, in His wicked and vile trial, the most unjust in the history of eternity, and in His crucifixion, the Father had to endure supreme agony of heart.

This was the price for our miserable sins. It would seem impossible for any man or woman to reject such love. Yet billions today live lives uncommitted to the One who evidences such love for them.

Let us ever remember the inspired words of Christ's step-brother:

> Every good gift and every perfect gift is from above, and cometh down from the Father of lights, with whom is no variableness, neither shadow of turning. Of his own will begat he us with the word of truth, that we should be a kind of firstfruits of his creatures. (James 1:17–18)

James also provides us with the appropriate response for us to make to our God.

> Wherefore, my beloved brethren, let every man be swift to hear, slow to speak, slow to wrath: for the wrath of man worketh not the righteousness of God. Wherefore lay apart all filthiness and superfluity of naughtiness, and receive with meekness the engrafted word, which is able to save your souls. But be ye doers of the word, and not hearers only, deceiving your own selves. For if any be a hearer of the word, and not a doer, he is like unto a man beholding his natural face in a glass: for he beholdeth himself, and goeth his way, and straightway forgetteth what manner of man he was. But whoso looketh into the

perfect law of liberty, and continueth therein, he being not a forgetful hearer, but a doer of the work, this man shall be blessed in his deed. If any man among you seem to be religious, and bridleth not his tongue, but deceiveth his own heart, this man's religion is vain. Pure religion and undefiled before God and the Father is this, To visit the fatherless and widows in their affliction, and to keep himself unspotted from the world. (James 1:19–27)

This is the wonderful Father we present to each reader. Love Him! Serve Him! Adore Him! Seek Him! Treasure His Word! Undertake His will! Above all choose to spend eternity with Him as offered in His free gift, remembering that

God is love. (1 John 4:8)

In the greatest sermon ever preached—our Savior's Sermon on the Mount, which embraces three chapters of the gospel of Matthew—Jesus continually reminded us of the Father's great love and compassionate care for us.

But I say unto you, Love your enemies, bless them that curse you, do good to them that hate you, and pray for them which despitefully use you, and persecute you; that ye may be the children of your Father which is in heaven: for he maketh his sun to rise on the evil and on the good, and sendeth rain on the just and on the unjust. (Matthew 5:44–45)

But thou, when thou prayest, enter into thy closet, and when thou hast shut thy door, pray to thy Father which is in secret; and thy Father which seeth in secret shall reward thee openly. But when ye pray, use not vain repetitions, as the heathen do: for they think that they shall be heard for their much speaking. Be not ye therefore like unto them: for your Father knoweth what things ye have need of, before ye ask him. (Matthew 6:6–8)

Behold the fowls of the air: for they sow not, neither do they reap, nor gather into barns; yet your heavenly Father feedeth them. Are ye not much better than they? Which of you by taking thought can add one cubit unto his stature? And why take ye thought for raiment? Consider the lilies of the field, how they grow; they toil not, neither do they spin: and yet I say unto you, That even Solomon in all his glory was not arrayed like one of these. Wherefore, if God so clothe the grass of the field, which to day is, and to morrow is cast into the oven, shall he not much more clothe you, O ye of little faith? Therefore take no thought, saying, What shall we eat? or, What shall we drink? or, Wherewithal shall we be clothed? (For after all these things do the Gentiles seek:) for your heavenly Father knoweth that ye have need of all these things. But seek ye first the kingdom of God, and his righteousness; and all these things shall be added unto you. (Matthew 6:26–33)

If ye then, being evil, know how to give good gifts unto your children, how much more shall your Father which is in heaven give good things to them that ask him? (Matthew 7:11)

Ponder these promises and trust in your Father. Christ's testimony to His Father greatly encourages us,

Fear not, little flock; for it is your Father's good pleasure to give you the kingdom. (Luke 12:32)

Index

Scripture References

People

Other Topics

Hartland Publications Book List

Note: This list is current as of the date of publication.
For an up-to-date list, please visit our web site at
http://www.hartlandpublications.com.

These books may be ordered from Hartland Publications
(see the last page of this book for complete contact information).
Many of these books are also available from Highwood Books in Australia: 03–59637011

Books by Colin Standish and Russell Standish
(Unless otherwise noted as by one or the other)

The Antichrist Is Here (187 pages)

A newly updated, second edition! Colin and Russell Standish have extensively researched the historical identification of the antichrist of past generations and are convinced the antichrist is present on earth now. They have taken those events which have transpired in the last decade and measured them in the light of biblical prophecy. You will read undeniable evidence in support of their findings. A "must-read" for those who are interested in biblical prophecy and its outworking in contemporary history.

The Big Bang Exploded (218 pages)

For decades the "big bang" hypothesis has held sway as the dominant explanation of the origin of the universe. It has proven to be a remarkably enduring hypothesis, yet the determined efforts of scientists from many disciplines have failed to provide confirmation of this hypothesis.

The authors assert that the "big bang theory" and Darwin's proposal of natural selection are "spent, decayed and archaic theories." The Standish brothers seriously address some of the most startling challenges to this theory of origins. They present evidence which they assert supports, far more closely, the fiat creation concept than the evolutionary model. This is another of the increasing challenges which evolutionary scientists must address if their credibility is not to be seriously undermined.

Education for Excellence (174 pages)

This book goes directly to the word of God for educational principles for the sons and daughters of the King of the Universe. In the ministry of the apostle Paul, the culture, philosophy and education of paganism was confronted by the principles of God-given education. Though the world of his day was under the political rulership of Rome, Greece still controlled the mind, and therefore the educational processes of the Mediterranean. As Paul's ministry led him to city after city under the influence of Greek education and philosophy, it was necessary for him to define clearly the differences between pagan and Christian education. Most cultures today face the continued influence of paganistic education. Many who claim to support Christian education nevertheless are not fully aware of the complete contrasts between the two. Christianity wholly defines the curriculum, the teacher selection, the teaching methodology, the extracurricular activities, etc. Its goals, purposes and objectives are entirely different from secular education.

The Entertainment Syndrome (118 pages)

This book explores how the large increase in entertainment impacts the physical, emotional, social, intellectual and spiritual life of the human race, and the devastating effect of its use in our churches.

The European Union, the North American Union, the Papacy, and Globalism (192 pages)

The book of Revelation reveals a powerful global movement just prior to the return of Christ—a moment which is deeply riveted in both politics and religion. They provide evidence that the Papacy is the religious backbone of this movement as it postures to become the superpower upon the planet. They explain the reason why this globalism will lead to the greatest tyranny this planet has ever witnessed and how every major unit of society will continue to support this globalism. The authors present evidence from biblical prophecy that this global thrust will not completely be achieved and how the world will be liberated from ruthless globalists.

The Evangelical Dilemma (222 pages)

There has never been a more urgent time for an honest review of the past, present and future of Evangelical Protestantism. The authors present an examination of the major doctrinal errors of Evangelical Protestants.

The Everlasting Gospel (368 pages)

This book is written for all sincere Christians of all faiths. The authors have been puzzled why so many Christians strongly believe "the gospel" and yet ignore the central theme of the gospel. The authors have preached this gospel on every inhabited continent of the world and now they present it in a fascinating, simply explained presentation in this book for all to understand and share with others.

Georgia Sits On Grandpa's Knee (R. Standish) (86 pages)

World-traveler Russell Standish delights in visiting with his little grand-daughter, Georgia. She loves to sit on her grandpa's knee and hear stories of "the old times" when her daddy was a little boy in Australia, Malaysia, Thailand, England, and Singapore. And it is Dr. Standish's delight to also share these tales of a family era now past—the joys of life together in exotic lands. Georgia thinks that other children will enjoy her grandpa's stories. Grandpa hopes so, too!

God's Solution for Depression, Guilt and Mental Illness (235 pages)

This powerful book argues with great persuasiveness that God is interested in every aspect of His created beings and that the perfect answers to man's needs are to be found in the Word of God.

Grandpa, You're Back! (R. Standish) (128 pages)

Pastor Russell Standish again delights and fascinates his granddaughter, Georgia, with stories of his many travels to countries ranging from South America to such far-flung places as Singapore, Africa, and beyond. These stories should pleasantly awaken the imagination of young readers.

Gwanpa and Nanny's Home (R. Standish and Ella Rankin) (128 pages)

"I am Ella Marie Rankin. I want to tell you about Gwanpa's and Nanny's home. But I have a problem! You see, I'm only three and I haven't yet learned to write. So, my Gwanpa is writing my story for me." So begins a book that Russell Standish wrote for his granddaughter.

Impossible Prophecies Fulfilled (160 pages)

The Koran of the Muslims and the writings of the Hindus, Buddhists, Shintoists, Taoists, and the Confucianists are conspicuously devoid of prophetic utterances. In contrast, the Bible has literally hundreds of prophecies. Many of these prophecies are rich in detail, unlike the prophecies of Nostradamus which are mystical and lacking in detail. There are prophecies built on time that are very specific. These prophecies defy the challenges of skeptics, agnostics, atheists, and those who follow non-Christian religions. The authors have chosen some of the most fascinating prophecies and have traced them to their pinpoint accuracy as revealed in history. This book is a must for infidels and Christians alike.

Liberty in the Balance (285 pages)

The bloodstained pathway to religious and civil liberty faces its greatest test in 200 years. The United States "Bill of Rights" lifted the concept of liberty far beyond the realm of toleration to an inalienable right for all citizens. Yet, for a century and a half, some students of the prophecies of John the Revelator have foretold a time just prior to the return of Christ when these most cherished freedoms will be wrenched from the citizens of the United States, and the U.S. would enforce its coercive edicts upon the rest of the world. This book traces the courageous battle for freedom, a battle stained with the lives of many martyrs.

The Lord's Day (317 pages)

In his famous encyclical *Dies Domini*, Pope John Paul II commenced with these words, "The Lord's Day—as Sunday was called from apostolic times. . . ." To many Protestants, this was an unexpected and much-approved declaration from the Roman Catholic supreme pontiff. The issue of the apostolic origin of Sunday-worship has often been a contentious one between Roman Catholics and Protestants. This book presents an in-depth examination of the Sabbath in the Scriptures.

Modern Bible Translations Unmasked (256 pages)

This fascinating book challenges the reader to consider two very serious problems with modern translations: first, the use of corrupted Greek manuscripts, and second, translational bias. The authors are deeply concerned about the paraphrases and some of the efforts to translate the Bible into colloquial language, but they are also deeply concerned about the more respected translations that are gaining great acceptance in today's society. You will learn how these modern translations are reinforcing false teachings and erroneous gospel presentations.

The Mystery of Death (144 pages)

There are those today who believe that the soul is immortal and externally preexisted the body. Pagan or Christian, the opinions vary widely. In this book, the history of these concepts is reviewed and the words of Scripture are investigated for a definitive and unchallengeable answer.

Perils of Ecumenism (416 pages)

The march of ecumenism seems unstoppable. From its humble roots after the first World War, with the formation of the Faith and Order Council at Edinburgh University, Scotland, and the Works and Labor Council at Oxford University, England, to the formation of the World Council of Churches in 1948 in Amsterdam, it has gained breathtaking momentum. The authors see the ecumenical movement as very clearly identified in

Holy Scriptures as the movement devised by the arch-deceiver to beguile the inhabitants of the world.

The Pope's Letter and Sunday Laws (116 pages)

The authors examine the biblical foundations upon which the pope seeks to buttress his apostolic letter, *Dies Domini*. But even the undoubted skill of the pope and his scholarly advisors cannot mask the fallacies of the pope's conclusions. The authors show emphatically that the pope's assertions are in deep contradiction to the record of the Holy Bible and that of history.

Postmodernism and the Decline of Christianity (160 pages)

Like stealth in the night, postmodernism has not only invaded the world but the church. It is a concept in which there are no universal laws, no ultimates, no immutables. It is a belief which developed out of the modernist world, though it has gone far beyond modernism. It is based upon the feelings of each individual. Truth is nothing more than the whims of each individual. Few Christians have understood the postmodernist agenda, let alone the profound influence it has exerted upon the Christian church. This book exposes how far this influence has invaded the portals of the Christian establishments and how it is destroying the very fabric of society.

The Rapture and the Antichrist (288 pages)

This book sets forth the plainest truths of Scripture directing Protestantism back to its biblical roots. It will challenge the thinking of all Christians, erase the fictions of the *Left Behind* Series, and plant the reader's spiritual feet firmly on the platform of Scripture.

The Rapture, the End Times and the Millennium (378 pages)

This book will open the minds of the readers to a clear understanding of areas of the end-time which have led to much perplexity among laypeople and theologians alike. It is also guaranteed to dispel many of the perplexities presently confronting those who are searching for a clear biblical exposition of the last cataclysmic days in which we now live.

The Second Coming (80 pages)

The Apostle Paul refers to the second coming of Jesus as the blessed hope. (Titus 2:12) Yet, soon after the death of all the apostles, doubts and debates robbed the people of this assurance and brought in the pagan notion of immediate life after death. In this new updated work, Colin and Russell Standish present a "wake-up call" for every complacent Christian.

Two Beasts, Three Deadly Wounds and Fifteen Popes (334 pages)

Revelation 13 presents two incomprehensible beasts—one of which received a deadly wound in one of its heads. Prophecy stated that this mortal injury would be healed, and that the power represented by the beast would be admired worldwide. The authors give a detailed history of the fifteen popes who have sat upon the papal throne since the infliction of the deadly wound. The reader will find compelling evidence that the deadly wound is now so well-healed that there remains virtually no trace of the scar. For students of Scripture, this book will enlighten and bring an understanding of biblical prophecy and perhaps a new appreciation of the conclusive accuracy of Bible prophecy. The authors present this book as for all minds, a challenge to all hearts, and a timely wake-up call for humanity.

Uncle Russell and Daddy Stories (208 pages)

When Colin's children, Nigel and Alexandra, were growing up, he frequently told them stories and lessons gleaned from events in the life of Colin and his twin brother Russell during the time they were boys and youth growing up in Australia. These stories included the surprise birth of Colin and Russell, some of the challenges of the depression years, up to their college graduation. Although the stories are not always flattering to two boys born into a very poor but deeply dedicated family, they provide unique, first-hand insights into the happenings and events which were to lay the foundation for a lifetime of service for the Saviour.

The Vision and God's Providences (C. Standish): Abridged (176 pages)

The story of the development of Hartland Institute must be attributed to God alone. Yet, many men and women have had the privilege of being

His humble instruments to contribute to Hartland's establishment. This book recalls divine leadings, human weakness, misunderstandings, and strong differences of opinion, and we cannot but wonder what God might have accomplished, had we listened perfectly to His voice.

Youth, Are You Preparing for Your Divorce? (168 pages)

A majority of youth, including Christian youth, are destined for divorce. Yes, you read this correctly! Unbeknown to them or to their parents, long before marriage or even courtship, the seeds of divorce have been sown to later produce their baneful consequences. Many youth who think they are preparing for marital bliss are preparing for divorce and, all too frequently, their parents are co-conspirators in this tragedy. The authors provide amazing simple principles to avert the likelihood of future divorce.

Youth Do You Dare! (C. Standish) (88 pages)

If you are a young person looking for workable answers to the many issues that confront you today, this book is for you. It presents a call to young people to follow truth and righteousness, and to live morally upright lives.

Other Books from Hartland Publications

Behold the Lamb—David Kang (107 pages)

God's plan of redemption for this world and the preservation of the universe is revealed in the sanctuary which God constructed through Moses. This book explains the sanctuary service in the light of the Christian's personal experience. Why this book? Because Jesus is coming soon!

Christ and Antichrist—Samuel J. Cassels (348 pages)

First published in 1846 by a well-known Presbyterian minister, who called this book "not sectarian, but a Christian and Protestant work." He hoped that the removal of obstacles might result in a more rapid spread of the Gospel. One of these obstacles he saw as "Antichristianity," a term he that he used to describe the Papal system.

Distinctive Vegetarian Cuisine—Sue M. Weir (326 pages)

100% vegan cooking, with no animal products—no meat, milk, eggs, cheese, or even honey. No irritating spices or condiments are used. Most of the ingredients can be found at your local market. There are additional nutritional information and helpful hints. Make your dinner table appealing to the appetite!

Food for Thought—Susan Jen (159 pages)

Where does the energy which food creates come from? What kinds of foods are the most conductive to robust health and well being in all dimensions of our life? What is a balanced diet? Written by a healthcare professional, this book examines the food we prepare for our table.

Group Think—Horace E. Walsh (96 pages)

Find out how a state of groupthink (or group dynamics) has often contributed to disaster in secular and spiritual matters, like the role of Hebrew groupthink in the rejection and ultimate crucifixion of the Son of God. Or, the Ecumenical Movement that seeks to unite the minds of dedicated men so much that their passion is to build one great super church following Rome.

Heroes of the Reformation—Hagstotz and Hagstotz (307 pages)

This volume brings together a comprehensive picture of the leaders of the Reformation who arose all over Europe. The authors of this volume have made a sincere endeavor to bring the men of Protestantism alive in the hearts of this generation.

The History of Protestantism—J. A. Wylie (2,136 pages)

This book pulls back the divine curtain and reveals God's hand in the affairs of His church during the Protestant Reformation. Your heart will be stirred by the lives of Protestant heroes, and your mind captivated by God's simple means to counteract the intrigues of its enemies. As God's church faces the last days, this compelling book will appeal and will be a blessing to adults as well as children.

History of the Reformation of the 16th Century—J. d'Aubigné (1,472 pages)

In history and in prophecy, the Word of God portrays the long continued conflict between truth and error. Today, we see an alarming lack of understanding in the Protestant Church concerning the cause and effect of the Reformation. This reprinted masterpiece pulls back the curtain of history and divine providence to reveal the true catalyst for the Reformation—God's Word and His Holy Spirit.

History of the Reformation in the Time of Calvin—d'Aubigné (2,039 pages)

The renovation of the individual, of the Church, and of the human race, is the theme. This renovation is, at the same time, an enfranchisement; and we might assign, as a motto to the Reformation accomplished by Calvin, as well as to apostolic Christianity itself, these words of Jesus Christ: The truth shall make you free. (John 8:32)

The Method of Grace—John Flavel (458 pages)

In this faithful reprint, John Flavel thoroughly outlines the work of God's Spirit in applying the redemptive work of Christ to the believer. Readers will find their faith challenged and enriched. In true Puritan tradition, a clearly defined theology is delivered with evangelistic fervor, by an author urgently concerned about the eternal destiny of the human soul.

The Reformation in Spain—Thomas M'Crie (272 pages)

The boldness with which Luther attacked the abuses and the authority of the Church in Rome in the 16th Century attracted attention throughout Christendom. Luther's writings, along with the earlier ones of Erasmus, gained a foothold with a Spanish people hungry for the truth. Thomas M'Crie makes a case for a Spain free of the religious errors and corruptions that ultimately dried up the resources and poisoned the fountains of a great empire.

Romanism and the Reformation—H. Grattan Guinness (217 pages)

The Reformation of the 16th Century, which gave birth to Protestantism, was based on Scripture. It gave back to the world the Bible. Such

Reformation work needs to be done again today. The duty of diffusing information on the true character and history of "Romanism and the Reformation" is one that presses on God's faithful people in these days.

Strange Fire—Barry Harker (209 pages)

The Olympic games are almost universally accepted as a great international festival of peace, sportsmanship, and friendly competition. Yet, the games are riddled with conflict, cheating, and objectionable competitiveness. Discover the disturbing truth about the modern Olympics and the role of Christianity in the rise of this neo-pagan religion.

Truth Triumphant—Benjamin George Wilkinson (438 pages)

The prominence given to the "Church in the Wilderness" in the Scriptures establishes without argument its existence and emphasizes its importance. The same challenges exist today with the Remnant Church in its final controversy against the powers of evil to show the holy, unchanging message of the Bible.

Who Are These Three Angels?—Jeff Wehr (126 pages)

The messages of three holy angels unfold for us events that are soon to take place. Their warning is not to be taken lightly. They tell of political and religious movements that signal the soon return of Jesus.

True Education History Series
from Hartland Publications

Livingstone-The Pathfinder—Basil Matthews (112 pages)

Like most boys and girls, David Livingstone wondered what he would become when he grew up. He had heard of a brave man who was a missionary doctor in China. He also learned that this Dr. Gulztoff had a Hero, Jesus, who had come to people as a healer and missionary. David learned all about this great Physician, and felt that the finest thing in the whole world for him was to follow in the same way and be a medical missionary. That was David's quest, which was his plan. Between these pages, you shall see how he made his good wish come true.

*Missionary Annals—Memoir of Robert Moffat—*M. L. Wilder (64 pages)

Robert Moffat first heard from his wise and pious mother's lips that there were heathen in the world and of the efforts of Christians sharing the knowledge of a Saviour who could raise them out of their base degradation. An intense desire took possession of him to serve God in some marked manner but how that would be, he did not know. Through a series of providential circumstances and in God's good time, the London Society accepted him as one of their missionaries, and in 1816, he embarked on his first trip and got his first glimpse of heathen Africa. This book will inspire the young and old as you read the many trials, disappointments, triumphs, and wondrous miracles that God can accomplish when one is fully surrendered to Him.

*The Waldenses—*The Church in the Wilderness (68 pages)

The faithful Waldenses in their mountain retreats were married in a spiritual sense to God who promised, "I will betroth thee unto me in faithfulness and thou shalt know the Lord." (Hosea 2:20) No invention of Satan could destroy their union with God. Follow the history of these people as they are compared to the dedicated eagle parents.

About the Authors

COLIN and **RUSSELL STANDISH** were born in Newcastle, Australia, in 1933. They both obtained their teaching diplomas from Avondale College in 1951. They were appointed to one-teacher elementary schools in rural areas of New South Wales, each teaching for three years.

In 1958, both completed a major in history and undertook an honors degree in psychology at Sydney University in the field of learning theory. Colin went on to obtain his Master of Arts degree with honors in 1961 and his Doctor of Philosophy in 1964. His Masters Degree in Education was completed in 1967.

Russell graduated as a physician in 1964. Six years later he was admitted to the Royal College of Physicians (UK) by examination. He was elevated to the Fellowship of the Royal Colleges of Physicians in Edinburgh (1983) and Glasgow (1984).

In 1965, Colin was appointed chairman of the education department at Avondale College. Subsequently he held the posts of academic dean and president at West Indies College (1970–1973), chairman of the Department of Psychology, Columbia Union College (1974), president of Columbia Union College (1974–1978), and dean of Weimar College (1978–1983). He was invited to become the foundational president of Hartland Institute (1983–), which comprises a college, a lifestyle center, a publishing house, media services, and a world mission division.

As a consultant physician (internist), Russell has held the posts of deputy medical superintendent of the Austin Hospital, University of Melbourne (1975–1978), president of a hospital in Bangkok (1979–1984), medical director at Enton Medical Centre, England (1984–1986), and president of a Penang hospital (1986–1992). From 1992 to the time of his death May 2, 2008, he was speaker and editor for Remnant Herald.

They have co-authored more than forty-five books.

HARTLAND Publications was established in 1984 as a Bible-centered, self-supporting Protestant publishing house. We publish Bible-based books and produce media for Christians of all ages, to help them in the development of their personal characters, always giving glory to God in preparation for the soon return of our Lord and Savior, Christ Jesus. We are especially dedicated to reprinting significant books on Protestant history that might otherwise go out of circulation. Hartland Publications supports and promotes other Christian publishers and media producers who are consistent with biblical principles of truth and righteousness. We are seeking to arouse the spirit of true Protestantism, one that is based on the Bible and the Bible only, thus awakening the world to a sense of the value and privilege of the religious liberty that we currently enjoy.

Office hours (Eastern time):
Monday – Thursday: 9:00 a.m. to 5:00 p.m.
Friday: 9:00 a.m. to 12:00 noon

Payment must be in US dollars by check,
money order, or most credit cards.

You may order via mail, telephone, fax, e-mail, or on our web site:
Hartland Publications
PO Box 1, Rapidan, VA 22733 USA
Order line: 1-800-774-3566 / Fax: 1-540-672-3568
E-mail: sales@hartlandpublications.org
Web site: www.hartlandpublications.com